A SEASONAL
BOOK OF HOURS

A SEASONAL BOOK OF HOURS

MORNING AND EVENING PRAYER FOR
ADVENT, CHRISTMAS, LENT AND EASTER

WILLIAM G. STOREY

LITURGY
TRAINING
PUBLICATIONS

ACKNOWLEDGMENTS

Many of the prayers in this book have been translated from old Latin texts by the author; some are his original compositions. He has also adapted scripture for many of the antiphons, verses and responses.

Other texts come from published works. We are grateful to the many publishers and authors who have given permission to include their work. Every effort has been made to determine ownership of all texts and to make proper arrangements for their use. We will gladly correct in future editions any oversight or error brought to our attention.

Acknowledgments continued on page 330.

A SEASONAL BOOK OF HOURS © 2001 Archdiocese of Chicago: Liturgy Training Publications, 1800 North Hermitage Avenue, Chicago IL 60622-1101; 1-800-933-1800; fax 1-800-933-7094; e-mail orders@ltp.org. All rights reserved.

Visit our website at www.ltp.org.

This book was edited by Lorie Simmons and Gabe Huck. Carol Mycio was the production editor. The cover design is by Larry Cope, and the typesetting was done by Jim Mellody-Pizzato in Stempel Garamond and Trajan. Printed by Webcom in Toronto, Canada. The interior is based on a design created by Lisa Buckley.

Library of Congress Control Number: 2001098358

ISBN 1-56854-350-6

SEBKHR

Dedicated to Good Pope John (1958–1963) and his program of reform, renewal and reunion.

TABLE OF CONTENTS

INTRODUCTION: THE CHURCH'S YEAR OF GRACE

For those who have already been using my previous publication, *An Everyday Book of Hours,* many things in this book will look familiar. But *A Seasonal Book of Hours* offers a deeper immersion in the texts for Advent, Christmas, Lent, Triduum and Easter. The earlier book includes options for adapting prayer to the seasons and so it may be used any time, but those who use *A Seasonal Book of Hours* will now find its predecessor more appropriate for Ordinary Time. Used together, the two books offer rich resources for praying morning, evening and night prayer through-out the church year.

THE CHURCH'S YEAR OF GRACE

In order to keep the memory of Jesus alive and green, the early churches of the Mediterranean world created a Christian week. The first day of the week became the Lord's Day: the day of the resurrection, of Pentecost, and of the coming again in glory to judge the living and the dead. Its liturgical center was the celebration of the Lord's supper on the Lord's Day. The sixth day of the week (Friday) became the weekly memorial of the passion and death of Jesus, a day of fasting and special prayer. In direct continuity with the Jewish custom of morning and evening prayer, early churches also marked the dawn and sunset hours with worship. By the second century, then, Christians had developed patterns of prayer: daily psalms, praise and petition in the morning and evening and the weekly observances of Sunday and Friday.

During this time churches also began to observe an annual Passover each spring to enter into the full paschal mystery—the incarnation, passion, death and resurrection of the Lord. In many churches this Easter celebration was held on March 25, regardless of the day of the week on which it fell. After considerable controversy most churches determined that the Pasch should be celebrated on a Sunday, the original day on which Christians had observed it. The first ecumenical Council of Nicea (325) fixed the date of Easter on the first Sunday after the first full moon following the spring equinox.

The annual celebration of the Christian Passover was the beginning of what would become a complete liturgical year. At the end of the period of overt persecutions in the early fourth century, the Christian year developed two focal points: Easter and Christmas. Easter, *pascha* in Latin, became a season of 50 days to feast and rejoice, culminating in the feast of Pentecost. In the fourth century the church created a season of preparation for Easter which we call Lent. For 40 days those who were to be baptized during the great Easter Vigil were prepared for their Christian initiation by prayer, instruction, fasting and exorcism. It also became a season of penance for those who had seriously violated the vows of their baptism and wanted to be readmitted to full church membership at Easter. Lent and Easter became—and remain—the very center of the liturgical year.

A second focus of the liturgical year emerged in the fourth or fifth century in all the churches of East and West. It focused on the feasts celebrating Christ's first manifestations in the world: Christmas, Epiphany, the Baptism of the Lord, the Presentation in the Temple. The Latin church developed a time of preparation for this festive season. We call it Advent. Through the holy words and symbols of the liturgy we prepare to welcome Christ coming again in humility, and we anticipate his second coming in glory. In the earliest surviving calendar of the Roman church (336), Christmas Day on December 25 marked the beginning of the liturgical year, but when Advent developed somewhat later, the year opened with the first Sunday of Advent.

As these two cycles of feasts and fasts were established, appropriate texts from the Bible and other sources were selected for the seasonal celebrations of the eucharist and the daily hours of prayer.

THIS BOOK OF HOURS

In line with the desire of the Second Vatican Council to restore the daily celebration of the Liturgy of the

Hours, *A Seasonal Book of Hours,* like its companion, *An Everyday Book of Hours,* presents a simplified and briefer version of Morning Prayer and Evening Prayer, but crafted especially for the four seasons of the liturgical year: Advent, Christmas, Lent and Easter, as well as for the Triduum. Those who have used *An Everyday Book of Hours* will be familiar with the format.

Each hour has the same structure:

- opening verses

- an optional hymn

- a psalm with antiphon, silent prayer and a psalm prayer

- a short reading from scripture with silence and a verse response

- a canticle

- intercessions (in the evening)

- the Lord's Prayer

- a concluding prayer

- a final blessing

This prayer book is arranged so that it may be used by groups as well as by individuals. Some people pray with their households or other associates. Such a group is an *ecclesiola* or little church; that is, a group of believers celebrating who they are and who Christ is for them (Acts 2:46–47). Other Christians pray the daily hours by themselves in their own rooms (Matthew 6:1, 5–6), a chapel or any other place. They should never forget that by virtue of their baptism they are full members of the world-wide church, the communion of saints, and they assemble, at least in spirit, with the whole church in heaven and on earth.

HOW TO PRAY THIS BOOK

FOLLOWING THE SCRIPT

For each season except Christmas you will find a week-long cycle of prayer that can be repeated as long as the season lasts. (Christmas is arranged with shorter cycles.) In the seasons (as in Ordinary Time), Sunday, the Lord's Day, holds a special position. Its celebration begins with Saturday Evening Prayer.

This book provides a kind of "script" for each morning and evening of the cycle. In the opening verses of the script a small cross [+] reminds you to sign your lips with this traditional gesture as you begin the hour. The same cross will appear in the closing verses when you sign your entire body.

Most of the texts are given in the script, but a few are not. The hymn, a traditional element in morning and evening prayer, is optional. It may be chosen from those located on pages 310–321. The Lord's Prayer and

Apostles' Creed (occurring later in the hour) are indicated by title only. Look for their full texts in the Basic Prayers section, pages 322–329.

The italicized verse after the title of the psalm or canticle is an antiphon (refrain). Taken usually from the New Testament or the psalm itself, it offers a focus point for the scripture. The antiphon is meant to be recited at the beginning and end of the psalm or canticle.

When more than one person prays morning or evening prayer together, a leader usually alternates speaking parts with the group. In this book the symbol [~] has been used to indicate the group's response to the leader's part—in opening verses, responses to the readings, intercessions, psalm prayer and closing blessings. When praying the psalm prayer, the leader customarily begins by saying, "Let us pray" and then pauses to allow time for the group's silent prayer before reciting the prayer text.

Someone other than the leader usually proclaims the scripture reading. Psalms and canticles are recited by all or by some simple form of alternating between the leader and the group.

THE TEXTS IN THIS BOOK

Traditionally, scripture readings for Morning Prayer and Evening Prayer come mainly from the Old Testament and epistles. Outside of the Canticles of Zachary and of Mary, the gospels appear only in brief phrases in the antiphons and responses. But this book presents a wider variety of texts. Canticles and scripture readings are drawn from all parts of the Bible, and a few Catholic classics outside of scripture serve as canticles. Many of the intercessions and other prayers have been gathered from throughout the Christian tradition; a number of texts were composed or translated by the author.

In the psalms when the word *Lord* appears in small capitals (LORD) it represents the unutterable name for God appearing in the Hebrew text as YHWH, sometimes translated as Yaweh.

YOUR SETTING FOR MORNING AND EVENING PRAYER

Choose the most conducive space for your daily prayer. Households may wish to gather around their table, just before or after breakfast and dinner. Other small groups might arrange themselves antiphonally (facing each other), creating two parts (choirs) for reciting the psalms.

Whether praying in a group or alone, you will feel more prayerful with a little attention to the environment—perhaps some sacred images or objects, a family Bible, candles. (Children love to light candles, and so do most adults.) Marking the liturgical seasons and feasts with green, purple, white, red or gold and other festive colors invites us into the sacred time of the church year.

When You Pray Alone

- Before beginning to pray morning or evening prayer, make a serious personal effort to stand in silence in the presence of the Holy Trinity: our Creator, Redeemer and Sanctifier. By grace God dwells in the depth of each soul, and by baptism each person is empowered to call on God as Abba, dear Father; on Jesus, our Lord and Savior; and on the Holy Spirit, our advocate and guide. With loving attentiveness we must try to be present to the indwelling God, and with a keen desire we must continue, day after day, to seek God's face.

- After a few moments of silence, recite the opening verses while making the sign of the cross on your lips.

- If you wish, sing or recite the hymn of the day from the Hymns section at the end of the book.

- Recite the psalm aloud with attention and devotion. The antiphon is usually recited just before and just after the psalm but, for further emphasis, it may be inserted between each stanza of the psalm. Antiphons are particularly helpful for relating the psalm texts to each season.

- After reciting the psalm, pause for a short time to reflect on the whole or some part of it so that its fuller meaning becomes more and more available and heartfelt. At the end of the pause, say the psalm prayer that interprets or applies the psalm.

- Read the short lesson from scripture, mull it over a bit, and listen to what God is saying to your heart through it. You may wish to substitute longer readings suggested in the Appendix (pages 306–329).

- After the reading and its pause for meditation, short seasonal verses lead into a biblical or devotional canticle with appropriate seasonal antiphons and a doxology.

- On Saturday evenings and Sunday mornings after the canticle we recite the Apostles' Creed, that prayerful affirmation of faith that renews the vows of our baptism.

- To conclude, pray the prayers of intercession (in the evening), the Lord's Prayer, closing prayer and blessing.

When You Pray in a Group

It is helpful to designate a leader of prayer and a reader of scripture. The leader of prayer

- calls the group to prayer with the opening verses and leads the hymn when it is used

- starts the psalm, then after a time of silence, prays the psalm prayer

- initiates the response after the reading and pauses for meditation

- leads the prayers of intercession, allowing time for spontaneous prayer at the end

- leads the recitation or chanting of the Lord's Prayer

- prays the closing prayer and asks the blessing

- if desired, invites a sign of peace at the end of evening prayer

The reader proclaims the brief lesson printed in the text or a longer reading from a Bible. (See the section Biblical Readings Throughout the Liturgical Year in the Appendix on page 307.) The reading may be introduced with the phrase, "A reading from the Book of . . ." At the end of the proclamation, the reader allows a pause and then concludes with, "The word of the Lord." All respond, "Thanks be to God."

Group Recitation of the Hymns, Psalms and Canticles

If the hymn is recited instead of sung, the leader may alternate reciting the stanzas of the hymn with the assembly. The poetry of the inspired psalms and canticles may be recited in these ways:

- The leader begins the antiphon and all join in. Then the leader alternates the psalm or canticle with the group stanza by stanza.

- The leader begins the antiphon and all join in. Then the group divides in two and alternates the stanzas of the psalm between the two choirs. The antiphon is repeated by all at the end of the psalm.

Postures and Gestures

Each individual or group will do what best fits its needs. For small group prayer it works well to stand for the opening verses and hymn, sit for the psalm, for the silence that follows it and the psalm prayer. Remain seated for the reading and its meditation period. Stand again for the canticle and for the Creed when it is used on Saturday evenings and Sunday mornings. The intercessions, Lord's Prayer, closing prayer and blessing may be prayed standing or kneeling. Make the sign of the cross while reciting the opening words of the canticles of Zachary and Mary and bow at the naming of the Holy Trinity in the doxologies.

Those who pray the hours by themselves are naturally free to adapt their style and stance to what is personally conducive to prayer, however these traditional practices can be very effective.

THE MOVEABLE FEASTS

January 1 is the beginning of the civil or secular year. The First Sunday in Advent is the beginning of the church's year and falls about four weeks before Christmas Day. Christmas is, of course, a fixed feast, but Ash Wednesday and Pentecost are both movable holy days and depend entirely on the date of Easter. By the decree of the Council of Nicea (325), Easter falls on the first Sunday following the first full moon after the spring equinox. It can occur as early as March 23 and as late as April 24.

If you do not have access to the dates of moveable feasts, call any local parish or the reference desk at your public library. You could also find a liturgical calendar online (for example, at the website of the archdiocese of New York, liturgyny.catholic.org).

It was John's mission—and greatness—to proclaim the advent of the kingdom of God. Nor was he in any way unworthy to do so, he who "even from his mother's womb" was filled with the Holy Spirit (Luke 1:15). It could only mean that his particular vocation was to lead the way to the promised realm, to direct others to it, but in some special sense to remain without. One is reminded of Moses close to death, standing on Mount Nebo and looking down on the Promised Land. He is not allowed to enter. Not until he has passed through death does he come into the true land of promise (Deuteronomy 34:1–6). For Moses this was punishment; he had failed in an hour of trial. For John it was not punishment but vocation. This side of death, John was to remain Precursor: herald of the kingdom.

~Romano Guardini

THE SEASON OF ADVENT

⚛

ADVENT'S PROPHETIC TEACHERS

Mighty figures from the scriptures confront us during the season of Advent. The prophet Isaiah, the "evangelist" of the Hebrew Scriptures, prepares Israel and us for the coming of the Messiah. Gabriel the archangel is the heaven-sent messenger who appears to Zachary the priest and announces that his wife, Elizabeth, will bear a son. That baby will become John the Baptist, the forerunner of the Messiah, who warns us to repent and change our hearts and minds to prepare the way of the Lord. Gabriel then appears to both Mary and Joseph and tells them to name their son Jesus. By December 24 we are ready for the singing angels announcing the Good News of Christ's birth, for the shepherds of Bethlehem and the Magi from afar with their precious, prophetic gifts for the babe on Mary's lap.

THE TWOFOLD COMING OF CHRIST

Saint Cyril of Jerusalem (ca. 315–386) points to another deep insight of the Advent season:

We do not preach only one coming of Christ, but a second as well, much more glorious than the first. The first coming was marked by patience; the second will bring the crown of a divine kingdom. In general, what relates to our Lord Jesus Christ has two aspects. There is a birth from God before the ages, and a birth from a virgin at the fullness of time. There is a hidden coming, like that of rain on fleece, and a coming before all eyes, still in the future. At the first coming he was wrapped in swaddling clothes in a manger. At this second coming he will be clothed in light as in a garment. In the first coming he endured the cross, despising the shame; in the second coming he will be in glory, escorted by an army of angels. We look then beyond the first coming and await the second.

RECKONING THE TIME

The season of Advent lasts four weeks and begins on the Sunday on or nearest the feast of Saint Andrew the Apostle (November 30). It comes to a close on December 24 with Morning Prayer of Christmas Eve.

SATURDAY EVENING

Light and peace **+** in Jesus Christ our Lord.
~*Thanks be to God.*

Let your face shine on us, O God.
~*And we shall be saved.*

HYMN

PSALM 48

See, the home of God is among mortals.

The LORD is great and worthy to be praised
in the city of our God,
whose holy mountain rises in beauty,
the joy of all the earth.

Mount Zion, true pole of the earth,
the Great King's city!
God, in the midst of its citadels,
is known to be its stronghold.

For the kings assembled together,
together they advanced.
They saw; at once they were astounded;
dismayed, they fled in fear.

A trembling seized them there,
like the pangs of birth.
By the east wind you have destroyed
the ships of Tarshish.

As we have heard, so we have seen
in the city of our God,
in the city of the LORD of hosts
which God upholds for ever.

God, we ponder your love
within your temple.
Your praise, O God, like your name
reaches the ends of the earth.

With justice your right hand is filled.
Mount Zion rejoices;
the people of Judah rejoice
at the sight of your judgments.

Walk through Zion, walk all round it;
count the number of its towers.
Review all its ramparts,
examine its castles,

that you may tell the next generation
that such is our God,
our God for ever and ever
will always lead us.

PSALM PRAYER

Lord of hosts,
you established your home in our midst
for the sake of all humanity.
As we ponder your love for us,
may we praise you with all our hearts
and tell the next generation
that you are our God for ever and ever.
~*Amen.*

READING   *Micah 2:12–13*

I will surely gather all of you, O Jacob, I will
gather the survivors of Israel; I will set them
together like sheep in a fold, like a flock in its
pasture; it will resound with people. The one
who breaks out will go up before them; they
will break through and pass the gate, going out
by it. Their king will pass on before them, the
LORD at their head.

SILENCE

RESPONSE

Christ shall stand and feed his flock:
~*In the strength of the Lord.*

CANTICLE OF MARY *Luke 1:46–55*

O Wisdom, O holy Word of God, permeating all creation: Come, and make us friends of God.

My soul + proclaims the greatness of the Lord,
my spirit rejoices in God my Savior,
for you, Lord, have looked with favor on your
    lowly servant.

From this day all generations will call me
    blessed:
you, the Almighty, have done great things for me
and holy is your name.
You have mercy on those who fear you,
from generation to generation.

You have shown strength with your arm
and scattered the proud in their conceit,
casting down the mighty from their thrones
and lifting up the lowly.
You have filled the hungry with good things
and sent the rich away empty.

You have come to the aid of your servant Israel,
to remember the promise of mercy,
the promise made to our forebears,
to Abraham and his children for ever.

Glory to the Father, and to the Son,
and to the Holy Spirit:
as it was in the beginning, is now,
and will be for ever. Amen.

APOSTLES' CREED

INTERCESSIONS

Blessed are you, Lord, God of our forebears:
~*Worthy to be praised and glorified for ever.*

Guide your church and keep it safe:
~*Hear us, O Lord.*

Give all nations peace and concord:
~*Hear us, O Lord.*

Grant us true repentance for our sins:
~*Hear us, O Lord.*

Strengthen us for perseverance in your service:
~*Hear us, O Lord.*

Grant us what we need for our daily life:
~*Hear us, O Lord.*

Reward with eternal life all those who do us
good for your name's sake:
~*Hear us, O Lord.*

Give a place of refreshment, light and peace
to the faithful departed:
~*Hear us, O Lord.*

Through the prayers of the Blessed Virgin Mary
and of the whole company of heaven:
~*Hear us, O Lord.*

LORD'S PRAYER

Let us pray as Jesus taught us:
~*Our Father . . .*

CLOSING PRAYER

Abba, dear Father,
help us to watch and pray eagerly
for the coming of our blessed Savior.
When he stands at the door and knocks,
may he not find us sleeping in our sins
but awake and expecting his return
as faithful servants and friends.
We ask this through the same Christ our Lord.
~*Amen.*

May the grace of our Lord Jesus Christ,
and the love of God and the communion of the
Holy Spirit, **+** be with us, now and for ever.
~*Amen.*

AN EVENING ANTHEM TO MARY DURING ADVENT

Mother of Christ,
our hope, our patroness,
star of the sea, our beacon in distress.
Guide to the shores of everlasting day
God's holy people on their pilgrim way.

Virgin, in you God made his dwelling place;
Mother of all the living, full of grace,
blessed are you: God's word you did believe;
"Yes" on your lips undid the "No" of Eve.

Daughter of God, who bore his holy One,
dearest of all to Christ, your loving Son,
show us his face, O Mother, as on earth,
loving us all, you gave our Savior birth.

The angel Gabriel brought the good news
to Mary.
~*And she conceived by the Holy Spirit.*

Abba, dear Father,
by the free consent of the Virgin Mary
you brought life and salvation
to all humanity.
Grant that we may experience
the power of her intercession
through whom we received the author of life,
our Lord Jesus Christ,
who lives and reigns with you
   and the Holy Spirit,
one God, for ever and ever.
~*Amen.*

May the Virgin Mary mild
+ bless us with her holy Child.
~*Amen.*

SUNDAY MORNING

O Lord, + open my lips.
~*And my mouth shall declare your praise.*

Blessed is the One who comes in the name
of the Lord.
~*Hosanna in the highest!*

HYMN

PSALM 19:2–7

You are the bright and the morning star,
O Christ our Lord.

The heavens proclaim the glory of God,
and the firmament shows forth the work
   of God's hands.
Day unto day takes up the story
and night unto night makes known the message.

No speech, no word, no voice is heard
yet their span extends through all the earth,
their words to the utmost bounds of the world.

There God has placed a tent for the sun;
it comes forth like a bridegroom coming
   from his tent,
rejoices like a champion to run its course.

At the end of the sky is the rising of the sun;
to the furthest end of the sky is its course.
There is nothing concealed from its burning heat.

Psalm Prayer

Abba, dear Father,
to enlighten the world
you sent us your Word
as the sun of truth and justice
shining on humanity.

Illumine our minds that we may discern
    your glory
and rejoice in the promise of your coming.
We ask this through the same Christ our Lord.
~*Amen.*

READING   *Romans 13:11–14*

Sisters and brothers, you know what time
it is, how it is now the moment for you to wake
from sleep. For salvation is nearer to us now
than when we became believers; the night is far
gone, the day is near. Let us then lay aside the
works of darkness and put on the armor of
light; let us live honorably as in the day. Let us
put on the Lord Jesus Christ.

SILENCE

RESPONSE

The Sun of righteousness shall rise:
~*With healing in his wings.*

CANTICLE OF ZACHARY   *Luke 1:68–79*

Lord, you will visit your people in peace.

Blessed are you, + Lord, the God of Israel,
you have come to your people and set them free.
You have raised up for us a mighty Savior,
born of the house of your servant David.

Through your holy prophets, you promised
    of old
to save us from our enemies,
from the hands of all who hate us,
to show mercy to our forebears,
and to remember your holy covenant.

This was the oath you swore
    to our father Abraham:
to set us free from the hands of our enemies,
free to worship you without fear,
holy and righteous before you,
all the days of our life.

And you, child, shall be called the prophet
    of the Most High,
for you will go before the Lord to prepare
    the way,
to give God's people knowledge of salvation
by the forgiveness of their sins.

In the tender compassion of our God
the dawn from on high shall break upon us,
to shine on those who dwell in darkness
    and the shadow of death,
and to guide our feet into the way of peace.

Glory to you, Source of all being,
Eternal Word, and Holy Spirit:
as it was in the beginning, is now,
and will be for ever. Amen.

APOSTLES' CREED

LORD'S PRAYER

Let us pray as Jesus taught us:
~*Our Father . . .*

CLOSING PRAYER

All-powerful God,
give us fresh strength for doing good
that Christ may find an eager welcome
   at his coming
and call us to his side in the kingdom of heaven,
where he lives and reigns with you
   and the Holy Spirit,
one God, for ever and ever.
~*Amen.*

May Jesus, the Lord of the living and the dead,
✛ bless us and keep us.
~*Amen.*

SUNDAY EVENING

Jesus Christ ✛ is the light of the world.
~*A light no darkness can extinguish.*

Show us your mercy, O Lord.
~*And grant us your salvation.*

HYMN

PSALM 85

Salvation is near for the God-fearing.

O LORD, you once favored your land
and revived the fortunes of Jacob,
you forgave the guilt of your people
and covered all their sins.
You averted all your rage,
you calmed the heat of your anger.

Revive us now, God, our helper!
Put an end to your grievance against us.
Will you be angry with us for ever,
will your anger never cease?

Will you not restore again our life
that your people may rejoice in you?
Let us see, O LORD, your mercy
and give us your saving help.

I will hear what the LORD has to say,
a voice that speaks of peace,
peace for his people and friends
and those who turn to God in their hearts.
Salvation is near for the God-fearing,
and his glory will dwell in our land.

Mercy and faithfulness have met;
justice and peace have embraced.
Faithfulness shall spring from the earth
and justice look down from heaven.

The LORD will make us prosper
and our earth shall yield its fruit.
Justice shall march in the forefront,
and peace shall follow the way.

PSALM PRAYER

God of mercy and fidelity,
you loved the world so much
that you sent us your only Son to be our Savior.
May we receive him as our Lord and brother
and celebrate his gracious coming
to inaugurate the reign of justice and peace.
We ask this in his holy name.
~*Amen.*

READING   *Philippians 4:4–7*

Brothers and sisters, Rejoice in the Lord always;
again I will say, Rejoice. Let your gentleness
be known to everyone. The Lord is near. Do
not worry about anything, but in everything by
prayer and supplication with thanksgiving let
your requests be made known to God. And the

peace of God, which surpasses all understanding, will guard your hearts and your minds in Christ Jesus.

SILENCE

RESPONSE

Hail Mary, full of grace, the Lord is with you.
~*Blessed are you among women.*

CANTICLE OF MARY *Luke 1:46–55*

O Lord of lords and Ruler of the house of Israel, who appeared to Moses in the burning bush and gave him the law on Sinai: Come, and save us.

My soul **+** proclaims the greatness of the Lord, my spirit rejoices in God my Savior,
for you, Lord, have looked with favor on your lowly servant.

From this day all generations will call me blessed:
you, the Almighty, have done great things for me and holy is your name.
You have mercy on those who fear you,
from generation to generation.

You have shown strength with your arm
and scattered the proud in their conceit,
casting down the mighty from their thrones
and lifting up the lowly.
You have filled the hungry with good things
and sent the rich away empty.

You have come to the aid of your servant Israel,
to remember the promise of mercy,
the promise made to our forebears,
to Abraham and his children for ever.

To the Ruler of the ages, immortal, invisible,
the only wise God,
be honor and glory, through Jesus Christ,
for ever and ever. Amen.

INTERCESSIONS

Let us call on Christ, the happiness
of all who wait for him:
~*Come, Lord, do not delay.*

Joyfully, we await your coming:
~*Come, Lord Jesus.*

You existed before all the ages:
~*Come, save us in this present age.*

You created the world and all who live in it:
~*Come, receive back the work of your hands.*

You came that we might have more abundant life:
~*Come, give us life eternal.*

You did not shrink from obedience unto death:
~*Come, snatch us from death's dominion.*

You came to gather all human beings into your embrace:
~*Come, show us your radiant face.*

By the prayers of the great Mother of God, Mary most holy, and of the whole company of heaven:
~*Hear us, O Lord, and have mercy on us.*

LORD'S PRAYER

CLOSING PRAYER

Creator and redeemer of humankind,
at your decree and by the consent of the Virgin
the Word took flesh in her womb.
May we come to share the divinity of Christ
who humbled himself by becoming human
   like one of us.
In Jesus' name we ask it.
~*Amen.*

May the peace of God,
which surpasses all understanding,
+ guard our hearts and minds in Christ Jesus
our Lord.
~*Amen.*

AN EVENING ANTHEM TO MARY DURING ADVENT, *page 9*

O Lord, **+** open my lips.
~And my mouth shall declare your praise.

Blessed is the One who comes in the name
of the Lord.
~Hosanna in the highest!

HYMN

PSALM 98

*All the ends of the earth have seen the salvation
of our God.*

Sing a new song to the LORD
who has worked wonders;
whose right hand and holy arm
have brought salvation.

The LORD has made known salvation;
has shown justice to the nations;
has remembered truth and love
for the house of Israel.

All the ends of the earth have seen
the salvation of our God.
Shout to the LORD, all the earth,
ring out your joy.

Sing psalms to the LORD with the harp
with the sound of music.
With trumpets and the sound of the horn
acclaim the King, the LORD.

Let the sea and all within it, thunder;
the world, and all its peoples.
Let the rivers clap their hands
and the hills ring out their joy

at the presence of the LORD, who comes,
who comes to rule the earth.
God will rule the world with justice
and the peoples with fairness.

PSALM PRAYER

God of love,
you have established Jesus your Son
as the sovereign peacemaker and reconciler.
Free the world to rejoice in his peace,
to glory in his justice, and to live in his love.
We ask this through the same Christ our Lord.
~Amen.

READING *Baruch 3:9, 13–14*

Hear the commandments of life, O Israel; give
ear, and learn wisdom! If you had walked in
the way of God, you would be living in peace
forever. Learn where there is wisdom, where

there is strength, where there is understanding,
so that you may at the same time discern where
there is length of days, and life, where there is
light for the eyes, and peace.

SILENCE

RESPONSE
They will see the Lord coming in the clouds,
alleluia.
~*With power and great glory, alleluia!*

CANTICLE OF ZEPHANIAH
Zephaniah 3:14–17a, 18–20

The Lord, your God, is in your midst.

Sing aloud, O daughter Zion;
shout, O Israel!
Rejoice and exult with all your heart,
O daughter Jerusalem!

The LORD has taken away the judgments
  against you,
he has turned away your enemies.
The king of Israel, the LORD, is in your midst;
you shall fear disaster no more.

On that day it shall be said to Jerusalem:
Do not fear, O Zion;
do not let your hands grow weak.
The LORD, your God, is in your midst,
a warrior who gives victory.

I will remove disaster from you,
so that you will not bear reproach for it.
I will deal with all your oppressors at that time.
And I will save the lame and gather the outcast,
and I will turn their shame into praise
and renown in all the earth.

At that time I will bring you home,
at the time that I gather you;
for I will make you renowned and praised
among all the peoples of the earth,
when I restore your fortunes
before your eyes, says the LORD.

Glory to God: Creator, Redeemer, and Sanctifier,
now and always and for ever and ever. Amen.

LORD'S PRAYER

CLOSING PRAYER

Lord our God,
prepare us for the coming of Christ your Son.
May he find us waiting in expectant prayer

for the full revelation of the children of God
through the same Christ our Lord.
~*Amen.*

May the Lord bless us and keep us.
~*Amen.*

May the Lord's face shine upon us.
~*Amen.*

May the Lord be gracious to us
and give **+** us peace.
~*Amen.*

MONDAY EVENING

The Lord **+** is my light and my salvation.
~*Whom shall I fear?*

Christ is coming in power and glory:
~*To judge the living and the dead.*

HYMN

PSALM 50:1–6, 8–15, 23

Our God comes and does not keep silence.

The God of gods, the LORD,
has spoken and summoned the earth,
from the rising of the sun to its setting.
Out of Zion's perfect beauty God shines.

Announced by devouring fire,
and surrounded by raging tempest,
God calls on the heavens and the earth
to witness the judgment of his people.

"Summon before me my people
who made covenant with me by sacrifice."
The heavens proclaim God's justice,
for God, indeed, is the judge.

"I find no fault with your sacrifices,
your offerings are always before me.
I do not ask more bullocks from your farms,
nor goats from among your herds.

For I own all the beasts of the forest,
beasts in their thousands on my hills.
I know all the birds in the sky,
all that moves in the field belongs to me.

Were I hungry, I would not tell you,
for I own the world and all it holds.
Do you think I eat the flesh of bulls,
or drink the blood of goats?

Offer to God your sacrifice;
to the Most High pay your vows.
Call on me in the day of distress.
I will free you and you shall honor me.
A sacrifice of thanksgiving honors me
and I will show God's salvation to the upright."

Psalm Prayer

Abba, dear Father,
your servant Jesus came to do your will
and pleased you more than all the holocausts
　　of old.
Accept the sacrifice of praise and thanksgiving
that we offer you through Christ and in Christ,
and perfect us in your service,
now and for ever.
~*Amen.*

READING　*Philippians 3:20–21*

Brothers and sisters, our citizenship is in heaven,
and it is from there that we are expecting a
Savior, the Lord Jesus Christ. He will transform
the body of our humiliation that it may be
conformed to the body of his glory, by the
power that also enables him to make all things
subject to himself.

Silence

RESPONSE

We are expecting a Savior from heaven:
~*Our Lord Jesus Christ.*

THE CANTICLE OF MARY   *Luke 12:46–55*

*Root of Jesse, standing as a signal to the peoples,
before whom all rulers are mute: Come and
save us; delay no longer.*

My soul **+** proclaims the greatness of the Lord,
my spirit rejoices in God my Savior,
for you, Lord, have looked with favor on your
    lowly servant.

From this day all generations will call me
    blessed:
you, the Almighty, have done great things for me
and holy is your name.
You have mercy on those who fear you,
from generation to generation.

You have shown strength with your arm
and scattered the proud in their conceit,
casting down the mighty from their thrones
and lifting up the lowly.
You have filled the hungry with good things
and sent the rich away empty.

You have come to the aid of your servant Israel,
to remember the promise of mercy,
the promise made to our forebears,
to Abraham and his children for ever.

Glory to the holy and undivided Trinity,
now and always and for ever and ever. Amen.

INTERCESSIONS

With confidence let us pray to Christ our
Redeemer who came to save all humanity:
~*Come, Lord Jesus.*

In the mystery of our flesh you revealed your
mission from the Father:
~*Give us new hope by your coming.*

You emptied yourself and became human
like one of us:
~*Show mercy toward us.*

By your first coming you gave us new life:
~*Free us from guilt when you come again.*

You are holy and strong and living for ever:
~*Bring us into our eternal inheritance.*

As you sit at the right hand of the Father:
~*Gladden the souls of the dead with the light
of your countenance.*

By the prayers of the Blessed Virgin Mary,
of Saint Joseph her spouse, and of all the saints:
~*Hear and help us, O Lord.*

LORD'S PRAYER

CLOSING PRAYER

Living and eternal God,
by the coming of our incarnate Savior,
free us from every trace of sin
and make us your faithful sons and daughters
in time and in eternity,
through the same Christ our Lord.
~*Amen.*

May the Word of God, full of grace and truth,
+ bless us and keep us.
~*Amen.*

AN EVENING ANTHEM TO MARY DURING ADVENT, *page 9*

TUESDAY MORNING

O Lord + open my lips.
~*And my mouth shall declare your praise.*

Blessed is the One who comes in the name
of the Lord.
~Hosanna in the highest!

HYMN

PSALM 100

*The earth will be full of the knowledge
of the Lord.*

Cry out with joy to the LORD, all the earth.
Serve the LORD with gladness.
Come before God, singing for joy.

Know that the LORD is God,
our Maker, to whom we belong.
We are God's people, sheep of the flock.

Enter the gates with thanksgiving,
God's courts with songs of praise.
Give thanks to God and bless God's name.

Indeed, how good is the LORD,
whose merciful love is eternal;
whose faithfulness lasts forever.

PSALM PRAYER

God, our dear Father,
maker and lover of peace,
to know you is to live,

to serve you is to reign.
Protect us from the violence and anarchy
    of our sins
and make us genuine disciples of the prince
    of peace,
who lives and reigns for ever and ever.
~*Amen.*

READING 1 *Thessalonians 5:2 – 5*

Brothers and sisters, you yourselves know
very well that the day of the Lord will come like
a thief in the night. When they say, "There is
peace and security," then sudden destruction will
come upon them, as labor pains come upon a
pregnant woman, and there will be no escape!
But you, beloved, are not in darkness, for
that day to surprise you like a thief; for you are
all children of light and children of the day.

SILENCE

RESPONSE

Let the clouds rain down the Just One.
~*And the earth bring forth a Savior.*

CANTICLE OF ISAIAH   *Isaiah 11:1–6, 9*

The child is called Wonderful Counselor, Mighty God, Everlasting Father, Prince of Peace.

A shoot shall come out from the stump of Jesse,
and a branch shall grow out of his roots.
The spirit of the LORD shall rest on him,
the spirit of wisdom and understanding,
the spirit of counsel and might,
the spirit of knowledge and the fear of the LORD.
His delight shall be in the fear of the LORD.

He shall not judge by what his eyes see,
or decide by what is ears hear;
but with righteousness he shall judge the poor,
and decide with equity for the meek of the earth;
he shall strike the earth with the rod
    of his mouth,
and with the breath of his lips he shall kill
    the wicked.
Righteousness shall be the belt around his waist,
and faithfulness the belt around his loins.

The wolf shall live with the lamb,
the leopard shall lie down with the kid,
the calf and the lion and fatling together,
and a little child shall lead them.

They will not hurt or destroy
on all my holy mountain;
for the earth will be full
of the knowledge of the LORD
as the waters cover the sea.

Glory to the Father, and to the Son,
and to the Holy Spirit:
as it was in the beginning, is now,
and will be for ever. Amen.

LORD'S PRAYER

CLOSING PRAYER

Gracious Father,
you show the world the splendor of your glory
in the coming of Christ, born of the Virgin.
Give us true faith and love
to celebrate the mystery of God made human.
We ask this through the same Christ our Lord.
~*Amen.*

May Christ, the Son of God and Mary,
+ bless us and keep us.
~*Amen.*

Light and peace **+** in Jesus Christ our Lord.
~*Thanks be to God.*

I will praise you, Lord my God, with all
my heart.
~*And glorify your name for ever.*

HYMN

PSALM 67

*Let the peoples praise you, O God; let all the
peoples praise you.*

O God, be gracious and bless us
and let your face shed its light upon us.
So will your ways be known upon earth
and all nations learn your saving help.

Let the peoples praise you, O God;
let all the peoples praise you.

Let the nations be glad and exult
for you rule the world with justice.
With fairness you rule the peoples,
you guide the nations on earth.

Let the peoples praise you, O God;
let all the peoples praise you.

The earth has yielded its fruit
for God, our God, has blessed us.
May God still give us blessing
till the ends of the earth stand in awe.

Let the peoples praise you, O God;
let all the peoples praise you.

PSALM PRAYER

Look on us with kindness, O Lord,
and make everyone know your power to save.
Help us to profess your holy name
with reverence and awe
and bring forth a harvest of good deeds.
In Jesus' name.
~*Amen.*

READING   *1 Thessalonians 5:6–8*

Sisters and brothers, let us not fall asleep as
others do, but let us keep awake and be sober;
for those who sleep sleep at night, and those
who are drunk get drunk at night. But since we
belong to the day, let us be sober, and put on
the breastplate of faith and love, and for a helmet
the hope of salvation.

SILENCE

RESPONSE

Let the clouds rain down the Just One.
~*And the earth bring forth a Savior.*

CANTICLE OF SIMEON *Luke 2:29–32*

*O Key of David and Scepter of the house of
Israel, when you open no one can shut, when
you shut no one can open: Come, proclaim
liberty to the prisoners who sit in darkness and
in the shadow of death.*

Now, + Lord, you let your servant go in peace:
your word has been fulfilled.

My own eyes have seen the salvation
which you have prepared in the sight
    of every people:

a light to reveal you to the nations
and the glory of your people Israel.

To the Ruler of the ages, immortal, invisible,
the only wise God,
be honor and glory, through Jesus Christ,
for ever and ever. Amen.

INTERCESSIONS

Let us pray to Christ our Savior,
the way, the truth, and the life:
~*Come and stay with us, Lord.*

Jesus, Son of the Most High, revealed
to the Virgin Mary by the angel Gabriel:
~*Come and rule your chosen people.*

Holy One of God, in whom John rejoiced
while still in his mother's womb:
~*Come and bring joy to all the earth.*

Jesus whose precious name was revealed
to Mary and Joseph by an angel:
~*Come and save your people from their sins.*

Light of the world, awaited by old Simeon
and by Anna the prophetess:
~*Come and comfort your people.*

LORD'S PRAYER

CLOSING PRAYER

Pour forth, O Lord,
your grace into our hearts
that we to whom the incarnation of Christ
your Son
was made known by the message of an angel,
may by his cross and passion
be brought to the glory of his resurrection,
through the same Christ our Lord.
~*Amen.*

May Christ our Savior,
coming on the clouds of heaven with great
power and glory, + bless us and keep us.
~*Amen.*

AN EVENING ANTHEM TO MARY DURING ADVENT, *page 9*

WEDNESDAY MORNING

O Lord, + open my lips.
~*And my mouth shall declare your praise.*

Blessed is the One who comes in the name
of the Lord.
~*Hosanna in the highest!*

HYMN

PSALM 145:1–13

*You are close to all who call you, who call on
you from their hearts.*

I will give you glory, O God my king,
I will bless your name for ever.

I will bless you day after day
and praise your name for ever.
You are great, LORD, highly to be praised,
your greatness cannot be measured.

Age to age shall proclaim your works,
shall declare your mighty deeds,
shall speak of your splendor and glory,
tell the tale of your wonderful works.
They will speak of your terrible deeds,
recount your greatness and might.
They will recall your abundant goodness;
age to age shall ring out your justice.

You are kind and full of compassion,
slow to anger, abounding in love.
How good you are, LORD, to all,
compassionate to all your creatures.

All your creatures shall thank you, O LORD,
and your friends shall repeat their blessing.
They shall speak of the glory of your reign
and declare your might, O God,

to make known to all your mighty deeds
and the glorious splendor of your reign.
Yours is an everlasting kingdom;
your rule lasts from age to age.

Psalm Prayer

Lord Jesus,
by your humble coming among us,
you established in our hearts
your gentle reign of justice, peace and love.
We praise and thank you for your loving-
kindness
and ask for the grace to praise your holy name
through all the ages of ages.
~Amen.

READING   *Isaiah 7:10–14*

The LORD spoke to King Ahaz and said, "Ask a
sign of the LORD your God; let it be deep as
Sheol or high as heaven." But Ahaz said, "I will
not ask and I will not put the LORD to the
test." Then Isaiah said: "Hear then, O house of
David! Is it too little for you to weary mortals,
that you weary my God also? Therefore the
Lord himself will give you a sign. Look, the
young woman is with child and shall bear a son,
and shall name him Immanuel."

Silence

Response

Drop down dew, O heavens, from above.
~And let the earth bud forth a Savior.

CANTICLE OF ZACHARY *Luke 1:67–7*

Hail, Mary, full of grace, the Lord is with you.

Blessed are you, ✛ Lord, the God of Israel,
you have come to your people and set them free.
You have raised up for us a mighty Savior,
born of the house of your servant David.

Through your holy prophets, you promised
    of old
to save us from our enemies,
from the hands of all who hate us,
to show mercy to our forebears,
and to remember your holy covenant.

This was the oath you swore
    to our father Abraham:
to set us free from the hands of our enemies,
free to worship you without fear,
holy and righteous before you,
all the days of our life.

And you, child, shall be called the prophet
    of the Most High,
for you will go before the Lord to prepare
    the way,
to give God's people knowledge of salvation
by the forgiveness of their sins.

In the tender compassion of our God
the dawn from on high shall break upon us,
to shine on those who dwell in darkness
    and the shadow of death,
and to guide our feet into the way of peace.

Glory to God: Creator, Redeemer, and Sanctifier,
now and always and for ever and ever. Amen.

LORD'S PRAYER

CLOSING PRAYER

Lord our God,
you have made the Virgin Mary
the model for all who welcome your word
and who put it into practice.
Open our hearts to receive it with joy,
and by the power of your Spirit
grant that we also may become a dwelling place
in which your Word of salvation is fulfilled.
We ask this through our Lord Jesus Christ,
    your Son,
who lives and reigns with you
    and the Holy Spirit,
one God, for ever and ever.
~*Amen.*

May the Word made flesh of the Virgin Mary
+ bless us and keep us.
~*Amen.*

Jesus Christ **+** is the light of the world.
~A light no darkness can extinguish.

Salvation is near for the God-fearing.
~And glory will dwell in our land.

HYMN

PSALM 24:7–10

Who shall stand in God's holy place?

O gates, lift high your heads;
grow higher, ancient doors.
Let the king of glory enter!

Who is the king of glory?
The LORD, the mighty, the valiant,
the LORD, the valiant in war.

O gates, lift high your heads;
grow higher, ancient doors.
Let the king of glory enter!

Who is the king of glory?
the LORD of heavenly armies.
This is the king of glory!

PSALM PRAYER

Lord Jesus, king of glory,
the Virgin Mother threw open the gates
   of her heart
to welcome the mystery of your divine
   intervention.
By her prayers, make us her children,
open to the Good News and to all that God
   asks of us.
You live and reign, now and for ever.
~*Amen.*

READING   *Luke 1:26–28, 31–32, 37–38b*

The angel Gabriel was sent by God to a town in Galilee called Nazareth, to a virgin engaged to a man whose name was Joseph, of the house of David. The virgin's name was Mary. And he came to her and said, "Greetings, favored one! The Lord is with you. And now you will conceive in your womb and bear a son, and you will name him Jesus. He will be great, and will be called the Son of the Most High, for nothing will be impossible with God." Then Mary said, "Here am I, the servant of the Lord; let it be with me according to your word."

SILENCE

RESPONSE

Blessed are you among women, O Virgin Mary, alleluia!
~*And blessed is the fruit of your womb, Jesus!*

THE CANTICLE OF MARY   *Luke 1:46–55*

O radiant Dawn, splendor of eternal light and sun of righteousness: Come, shine on those who dwell in darkness and in the shadow of death.

My soul **+** proclaims the greatness of the Lord,
my spirit rejoices in God my Savior,
for you, Lord, have looked with favor on your
    lowly servant.

From this day all generations will call me
    blessed:
you, the Almighty, have done great things for me
and holy is your name.
You have mercy on those who fear you,
from generation to generation.

You have shown strength with your arm
and scattered the proud in their conceit,
casting down the mighty from their thrones
and lifting up the lowly.
You have filled the hungry with good things
and sent the rich away empty.

You have come to the aid of your servant Israel,
to remember the promise of mercy,
the promise made to our forebears,
to Abraham and his children for ever.

Glory to God: Creator, Redeemer, and Sanctifier,
now and always and for ever and ever. Amen.

INTERCESSIONS

Let us pray to Christ, the joy of all who wait
for his coming:
~*Come, Lord Jesus.*

You existed before the ages of ages:
~*Come and save us in this present age.*

You made the world and all it contains:
~*Come and save the work of your hands.*

You assumed our humanity, doomed to death:
~*Come and save us from the bonds of the grave.*

You issued forth from a virginal womb:
~*Come and give fresh life to a fallen world.*

By the prayers of Saint Mary the Virgin and of
all the saints:
~*Hear us and have mercy.*

THE LORD'S PRAYER

CLOSING PRAYER

Eternal Father,
you have established in the Virgin Mary
the royal throne of your Wisdom.
Enlighten your church by the Word of life,
that we may walk in the splendor of truth
and come to the full knowledge of the mystery
  of your love,
through the same Christ our Lord.
~*Amen.*

May the Virgin Mary mild
+ bless us with her holy Child.
~*Amen.*

AN EVENING ANTHEM TO MARY DURING ADVENT, *page 9*

THURSDAY MORNING

O Lord, + open my lips.
~*And my mouth shall declare your praise.*

Blessed is the One who comes in the name
of the Lord.
~*Hosanna in the highest!*

HYMN

SONG OF ISAIAH   *Isaiah 35:1– 2, 5 –7, 10*

Hosanna to the Son of David!

The wilderness and the dry land shall be glad,
the desert shall rejoice and blossom;
like the crocus it shall blossom abundantly,
and rejoice with joy and singing.

The glory of Lebanon shall be given to it,
the majesty of Carmel and Sharon.
They shall see the glory of the LORD,
the majesty of our God.

Then the eyes of the blind shall be opened,
and the ears of the deaf unstopped;
then the lame shall leap like a deer,
and the tongue of the speechless sing for joy.

For waters shall break forth in the wilderness,
and streams in the desert;
the burning sand shall become a pool,
and the thirsty ground springs of water.

And the ransomed of the LORD shall return,
and come to Zion with singing;
everlasting joy shall be upon their heads;
they shall obtain joy and gladness,
and sorrow and sighing shall flee away

PSALM PRAYER

Majestic God,
at the coming of our Savior,
you give sight to the blind.
Unstop the ears of the deaf,
and make the dumb sing for joy.
Give us the courage you promise,
end the time of lament and sorrow,
and make our faces shine with gladness,
through the same Christ our Lord.
~*Amen.*

READING   *Isaiah 9:6–7*

A child has been born for us, a son given
to us; authority rests upon his shoulders; and
he is named Wonderful Counselor, Mighty
God, Everlasting Father, Prince of Peace. His
authority shall grow continually, and there
shall be endless peace for the throne of David
and his kingdom. He will establish and uphold
it with justice and with righteousness from
this time onward and forevermore.

SILENCE

RESPONSE

The people who walked in darkness:
~*Have seen a great light.*

CANTICLE OF ISAIAH
Isaiah 26:1–4, 7–8, 12

Lord, we acknowledge your name alone.

We have a strong city;
God sets up victory
like walls and bulwarks.
Open the gates,
so that the righteous nation that keeps faith
may enter in.

Those of steadfast mind you keep in peace—
in peace because they trust in you.
Trust in the LORD forever,
for in the LORD GOD
you have an everlasting rock.

The way of the righteous is level;
O Just One, you make smooth
the path of the righteous.
In the path of your judgments,
O LORD, we wait for you;
your name and your renown
are the soul's desire.

O LORD, you will ordain peace for us,
for indeed, all that we have done,
you have done for us.

Glory to the holy and undivided Trinity:
now and always and for ever and ever. Amen.

LORD'S PRAYER

CLOSING PRAYER

Loving Father,
you make all things new
in your anointed Son, our Savior.
May his coming free us from our sins
and bring us into fresh hope and joy,
for he is Lord, now and for ever.
~*Amen.*

May grace + be with all who have undying love
for our Lord Jesus Christ.
~*Amen.*

THURSDAY EVENING

The Lord + is my light and my salvation.
~*Whom shall I fear?*

Faithfulness shall spring from the earth.
~*And justice look down from heaven.*

HYMN

PSALM 147:1–11

The Lord delights in praise from the faithful.

Sing praise to the LORD who is good;
sing to our God who is loving:
to God our praise is due.

The LORD builds up Jerusalem
and brings back Israel's exiles,
God heals the broken-hearted,
and binds up all their wounds.
God fixes the number of the stars;
and calls each one by its name.

Our Lord is great and almighty;
God's wisdom can never be measured.
The LORD raises the lowly;
and humbles the wicked to the dust.
O sing to the LORD, giving thanks;
sing psalms to our God with the harp.

God covers the heavens with clouds,
and prepares the rain for the earth;
making mountains sprout with grass
and with plants to serve our needs.
God provides the beasts with their food
and the young ravens when they cry.

God takes no delight in horses' power
nor pleasure in warriors' strength.
The LORD delights in those who revere him,
in those who wait for his love.

PSALM PRAYER

Abba, dear Father,
heal the brokenhearted
and bandage up all their wounds;
provide the hungry with food,
and lift the humble from the dust.
We eagerly wait for your love
coming in and through Jesus our Lord,
who lives and reigns with you
    and the Holy Spirit,
now and for ever.
~Amen.

READING   *Jeremiah 23:5–6*

The days are surely coming, says the LORD,
when I will raise up for David a righteous
Branch, and he shall reign as king and deal
wisely, and shall execute justice and righteousness in the land. In his days Judah will be
saved and Israel will live in safety. And this is
the name by which he will be called: "The
LORD is our righteousness."

SILENCE

RESPONSE

Blessed is the womb that bore you, O Christ.
~*And the breasts that nursed you.*

CANTICLE OF ISAIAH   *Isaiah 5:1–4*

O long-expected Ruler of the nations, the
precious cornerstone that unites all peoples:
Come, and deliver those whom you fashioned
from the dust of the earth.

Let me sing for my beloved
my love-song concerning his vineyard:
My beloved had a vineyard on a very fertile hill.
He dug it and cleared it of stones,
and planted it with choice vines;
he built a watchtower in the midst of it,
and hewed out a vine vat in it;
he expected it to yield grapes,
but it yielded wild grapes.

And now, inhabitants of Jerusalem
and people of Judah,
judge between me and my vineyard.
What more was there to do for my vineyard
that I have not done in it?
When I expected it to yield grapes,
why did it yield wild grapes?

To the Ruler of the ages, immortal, invisible,
the only wise God,
be honor and glory, through Jesus Christ,
for ever and ever. Amen.

INTERCESSIONS

Let us pray to the Word made flesh,
the way, the truth, and the life:
~*Come and teach our hearts.*

In God we live and move and have our being:
~*Come and make us the people of God.*

You are not far from any one of us:
~*Reveal yourself to all who seek your face.*

Father of the poor and comforter of the afflicted:
~*Set prisoners free and give hope to the dying.*

You hate death and love life.
~*Free us from sin, death and hell.*

By the intercession of the Blessed Virgin Mary
and of the whole company of heaven:
~*Hear us, O Lord, and have mercy on us.*

LORD'S PRAYER

CLOSING PRAYER

Lord Jesus Christ,
by love's decree you became human
    like one of us

in order to establish a community of faith
    and fellowship.
Gather all nations and people into your church
and make it a city of justice and peace
for the good of the whole human family.
We ask this in your holy name.
~*Amen.*

May the Lord + bless us,
protect us from all evil,
and bring us to everlasting life.
~*Amen.*

AN EVENING ANTHEM TO MARY DURING ADVENT, *page 9*

FRIDAY MORNING

O Lord, + open my lips.
~*And my mouth shall declare your praise.*

Blessed is the One who comes in the name
of the Lord.
~*Hosanna in the highest!*

HYMN

PSALM 119:1-2, 4-8

I baptize you with water; he will baptize you
with the Holy Spirit and with fire.

They are happy whose life is blameless,
who follow God's law!
They are happy who do God's will,
seeking God with all their hearts.
You have laid down your precepts
to be obeyed with care.
May my footsteps be firm
to obey your statutes.
Then I shall not be put to shame
as I heed your commands.
I will thank you with an upright heart
as I learn your decrees.
I will obey your statutes;
do not forsake me.

PSALM PRAYER

Almighty God and Father,
deliver us by the long-awaited birth of your Son
from the yoke of sin and servitude
that still weighs us down,
and bring us into the freedom of the children
   of God.
We ask this through Christ our Lord.
~Amen.

READING *Luke 1:39–42, 57, 60, 80*

Mary set out and went with haste to a Judean
town in the hill country, where she entered
the house of Zechariah and greeted Elizabeth.
When Elizabeth heard Mary's greeting, the
child leaped in her womb. And Elizabeth was
filled with the Holy Spirit and exclaimed with
a loud cry, "Blessed are you among women,
and blessed is the fruit of your womb." Now
the time came for Elizabeth to give birth,
and she bore a son called John. The child grew
and became strong in spirit, and he was in
the wilderness until the day he appeared pub-
licly to Israel.

Silence

Response

You have raised up for us a mighty Savior:
~*Born of the house of your servant David.*

CANTICLE OF ISAIAH
Isaiah 40:3–5, 9–10a

*You, child, shall be called the prophet of the
Most High; for you will go before the Lord
to prepare the way.*

A voice cries out:
"In the wilderness
prepare the way of the LORD,
make straight in the desert
a highway for our God.

Every valley shall be lifted up,
and every mountain and hill be made low;
the uneven ground shall become level,
and the rough places a plain.

Then the glory of the LORD shall be revealed,
and all people shall see it together,
for the mouth of the LORD has spoken."

Get you up to a high mountain, O Zion,
herald of good tidings;
lift up your voice with strength, O Jerusalem,
herald of good tidings,
lift it up, do not fear;
say to the cities of Judah,
"Here is your God!"

Glory to the holy and undivided Trinity:
now and always and for ever and ever. Amen.

LORD'S PRAYER

CLOSING PRAYER

Jesus, Messiah of Israel,
at your first coming you sent your messenger
to prepare a way before you.
Stir up the preaching of the gospel
and turn our hearts to true repentance
that at your second coming to judge the world
we may be found an acceptable people.
For yours is the power and the glory
   for ever and ever.
~*Amen.*

May the God of the prophets and seers
+ bless us and keep us.
~*Amen.*

FRIDAY EVENING

Jesus Christ **+** is the light of the world.
~*A light no darkness can extinguish.*

The Lord is my light and my salvation.
~*Whom shall I fear?*

HYMN

PSALM 80:1-19

*God of hosts bring us back; let your face shine
on us and we shall be saved.*

O shepherd of Israel, hear us,
you who lead Joseph's flock,
shine forth from your cherubim throne
upon Ephraim, Benjamin, Manasseh.
O Lord, rouse up your might,
O Lord, come to our help.

God of hosts, bring us back;
let your face shine on us and we shall be saved.

LORD God of hosts, how long
will you frown on your people's plea?
You have fed them with tears for their bread,
an abundance of tears for their drink.
You have made us the taunt of our neighbors,
our enemies laugh us to scorn.

God of hosts, bring us back;
let your face shine on us and we shall be saved.

You brought a vine out of Egypt;
to plant it you drove out the nations,
Before it you cleared the ground;
it took root and spread through the land.

The mountains were covered with its shadow,
the cedars of God with its boughs.
It stretched out its branches to the sea,
to the Great River it stretched out its shoots.

Then why have you broken down its walls?
It is plucked by all who pass by.
It is ravaged by the boar of the forest,
devoured by the beasts of the field.

God of hosts, turn again, we implore,
look down from heaven and see.
Visit this vine and protect it,
the vine your right hand has planted.
They have burnt it with fire and destroyed it.
May they perish at the frown of your face.

May your hand be on the one you have chosen,
the one you have given your strength.
And we shall never forsake you again;
give us life that we may call upon your name.

Psalm Prayer

Gracious Guardian of your people,
you have nurtured the vineyard you planted
until it covers the face of the earth.
Help us to be as verdant branches in the vine,
that, firmly rooted in your love,

---

we may testify before the world to your
saving help.
We ask this through Christ our Lord.
~*Amen.*

READING   *Mark 1:1–5*

The beginning of the good news of Jesus the
Christ, the Son of God. As it is written in the
prophet Isaiah, "See, I am sending my messenger
ahead of you, who will prepare your way; the
voice of one crying out in the wilderness:
'Prepare the way of the Lord, make his paths
straight,'" John the baptizer appeared in the
wilderness, proclaiming a baptism of repentance
for the forgiveness of sins. And people from
the whole Judean countryside and all the people
of Jerusalem were going out to him, and were
baptized by him in the river Jordan, confessing
their sins.

SILENCE

RESPONSE

Prepare the way of the Lord.
~*Make straight the paths.*

CANTICLE OF MARY   *Luke 1:46–55*

*O Emmanuel, our ruler and our lawgiver, the
awaited of the nations and their Savior: Come,
and save us, O Lord our God.*

My soul + proclaims the greatness of the Lord,
my spirit rejoices in God my Savior,
for you, Lord, have looked with favor on your
    lowly servant.

From this day all generations will call me
    blessed:
you, the Almighty, have done great things for me
and holy is your name.
You have mercy on those who fear you,
from generation to generation.

You have shown strength with your arm
and scattered the proud in their conceit,
casting down the mighty from their thrones
and lifting up the lowly.
You have filled the hungry with good things
and sent the rich away empty.

You have come to the aid of your servant Israel,
to remember the promise of mercy,
the promise made to our forebears,
to Abraham and his children for ever.

Glory to the Father, and to the Son,
and to the Holy Spirit:
as it was in the beginning, is now,
and will be for ever. Amen.

INTERCESSIONS

Let us pray to Israel's Messiah
who was recognized by John the Baptist:
~*Lord, hear our prayer.*

Lord of the prophets and seers of Israel:
~*Lord, hear our prayer.*

Lord of those who warned and exhorted your
chosen people:
~*Lord, hear our prayer,*

Lord of Elizabeth and Zachary, the parents
of John:
~*Lord, hear our prayer.*

Lord of John the Baptist, the messenger you
sent before you:
~*Lord, hear our prayer.*

By the prayers of Saint Mary the Virgin
and of John the Baptist the forerunner:
~*Lord, hear our prayer.*

LORD'S PRAYER

CLOSING PRAYER

God of mercy and compassion,
you sent John the Baptist before your Son
in the spirit and power of Elijah the Prophet
to prepare a perfect people for yourself.
Pour out the gift of repentance on your people
and prepare us for the joy that is coming
in the birth of your beloved Son.
We ask this in the name of Christ our Savior.
~*Amen.*

May the Lord bless us and take care of us.
~*Amen.*

May the Lord be kind and gracious to us.
~*Amen.*

May the Lord look on us with favor and
+ grant us peace.
~*Amen.*

AN EVENING ANTHM TO MARY DURING ADVENT, *page 9*

SATURDAY MORNING

O Lord, **+** open my lips.
~*And my mouth shall declare your praise.*

Blessed is the One who comes in the name
of the Lord.
~Hosanna in the highest!

HYMN

PSALM 147:12–20

God has not dealt thus with other nations.

O praise the LORD, Jerusalem!
Zion, praise your God!

God has strengthened the bars of your gates,
and has blessed the children within you;
has established peace on your borders,
and feeds you with finest wheat.

God sends out word to the earth
and swiftly runs the command.
God showers down snow white as wool,
and scatters hoarfrost like ashes.

God hurls down hailstones like crumbs,
and causes the waters to freeze.
God sends forth a word and it melts them:
at the breath of God's mouth the waters flow.

God makes his word known to Jacob,
to Israel his laws and decrees.
God has not dealt thus with other nations;
has not taught them divine decrees.

Psalm Prayer

God of nature and of grace,
you provision the human race
and feed the children of your church
with the finest wheat from your table.
Send forth your word to melt our hard hearts,
unstop our ears to hear you speak
and teach us the spirit of the gospel,
through Jesus Christ our Lord.
~*Amen.*

READING   *Isaiah 61:1–2a, c*

Sisters and brothers, the spirit of the Lord
GOD is upon me, because the LORD has
anointed me; he has sent me to bring good
news to the oppressed, to bind up the
brokenhearted, to proclaim liberty to the
captives, and release to the prisoners; to
proclaim the year of the LORD's favor,
and to comfort all who mourn.

SILENCE

RESPONSE

The Lord God will cause righteousness
and praise:
~*To spring up before all the nations.*

CANTICLE OF ISAIAH   *Isaiah 61:10–11*

*The Holy Spirit will come upon you, O Mary,
and the power of the Most High will over-
shadow you.*

I will greatly rejoice in the LORD,
my whole being shall exult in my God;
for he has clothed me with the garments
    of salvation,
he has covered me with the robe of
    righteousness,
as a bridegroom decks himself with a garland,
as a bride adorns herself with her jewels.

For as the earth brings forth its shoots,
and as a garden causes what is sown in it
    to spring up,
so the LORD God will cause righteousness
    and praise
to spring up before all the nations.

To the Ruler of the ages, immortal, invisible,
the only wise God,
be honor and glory, through Jesus Christ,
for ever and ever. Amen.

LORD'S PRAYER

CLOSING PRAYER

Heavenly Father,
you appointed your only-begotten Son
to be the Savior of humanity
and told his parents to name him Jesus.
May we who call him Savior now
come to see him face to face in heaven,
where he lives and reigns with you
    and the Holy Spirit,
one God, for ever and ever.
~*Amen.*

May Christ Jesus, who is coming in glory
to judge the living and the dead,
+ bless us and keep us.
~*Amen.*

Return to page 3 for the second, third and fourth weeks of Advent.

Bethlehem, make ready, for Eden is opened for all.
Be alert, for the tree of life blossoms forth
from the Virgin in the cave.
Her womb has become a spiritual paradise
wherein the divine Fruit was planted;
if we eat it we shall live and not die like Adam
    and Eve.
Christ comes to bring back to life the likeness
    to God
that we had lost in the beginning.

~Byzantine Liturgy for Christmas

THE SEASON OF CHRISTMAS

ON REJOICING AT THE BIRTHDAY OF CHRIST

Hear what Saint Augustine (354–430) preached:

> So then, let us celebrate the birthday of the Lord with all due festive gatherings. Let men rejoice, let women rejoice. Christ has been born, a man; he has been born of a woman; and each sex has been honored. Now therefore, let everyone, having been condemned in the first man, pass over to the second. It was a woman who sold us death; a woman who bore us life. "The likeness of the flesh of sin" (Romans 8:3) has been born, so that the flesh of sin might be cleansed and purified. And thus it is not the flesh that is to be faulted, but the fault that must die in order that the nature may live; because one has been born without fault, in whom the other who was at fault may be reborn. . . . Rejoice, you just, (Psalm 33:1); it is the birthday of the Justifier. Rejoice, you who are weak and sick; it is the birthday of the Savior, the Healer. Rejoice, captives; it is the

birthday of the Redeemer. Rejoice, slaves; it is the birthday of the one who makes you lords. Rejoice, free people; it is the birthday of the one who makes you free. Rejoice, all Christians; it is the birthday of Christ.

RECKONING THE TIME

The celebration of the nativity of the Lord Jesus began in the city of Rome shortly after the end of the last wave of Roman persecutions and during the reign of the Emperor Constantine (306–337). At a much earlier period it had been agreed that Jesus had been conceived by Mary and also had died on March 25, the spring equinox. This made the symbolic date of his birth to be December 25, the winter solstice. Very shortly this new feast spread to all the Latin churches and before long to those of the East as well. It proved to be the beginning of a whole season of feasts celebrating the incarnation and manifestation of the Word of God to Israel and to the world.

The season of Christmas begins with Evening Prayer on December 24. Although the official church calendar now ends the Christmas season with the Baptism of the Lord, traditionally the season extended through Evening Prayer of the Presentation of the Lord (February 2).

SOLEMNITIES AND FEASTS WITHIN THE CHRISTMAS SEASON

January 1, the Solemnity of Mary, the Mother of God, is the oldest festival of Mary in the Roman liturgy. On the final day of the octave of Christmas, we celebrate the virginal and divine motherhood of Mary our mother and our adoption through Jesus as the children of God who are authorized to address God as Abba, dear Father.

Since the fourth or fifth century, Epiphany, the feast of the appearance of God, has been observed on January 6 in both Eastern and Western calendars, but in Canada and the United States it is now kept on the Sunday that falls between January 2 and 8. In most years, the feast of the Baptism of the Lord is celebrated on the first Sunday after Epiphany.

The Presentation of the Lord on February 2 brings to a close the mysteries of the Christmas-Epiphany season. It is primarily a feast of our Lord and secondarily a feast of Mary, sometimes called Lady Day or Candlemas. Forty days after his birth, the parents of Jesus bring him to the Jerusalem temple to present their firstborn to the Lord. Old Simeon and the prophetess Anna recognize and proclaim Jesus as the long-awaited Messiah of Israel and as the light of the Gentile world. This is the final recognition feast of the Christmas cycle.

Light and peace **+** in Jesus Christ our Lord.
~*Thanks be to God.*

The glory of the Lord shall be revealed.
~*And all people shall see the glory of our God.*

HYMN

SONG OF ISAIAH   *Isaiah 52:7–10*

*Tomorrow salvation shall be yours, says the
Lord of hosts.*

How beautiful upon the mountains
are the feet of the messenger
who announces peace,
who brings good news,
who announces salvation,
who says to Zion, "Your God reigns."

Listen! Your sentinels lift up their voices,
together they sing for joy;
for in plain sight they see
the return of the LORD to Zion.

Break forth together in singing,
you ruins of Jerusalem;
for the LORD has comforted his people,
and has redeemed Jerusalem.

The LORD has bared his holy arm
before the eyes of all the nations;
and all the ends of the earth
shall see the salvation of our God.

PSALM PRAYER

Abba, dear Father,
as we celebrate your Son's birth in the flesh,
grant that we who receive him as our Savior
may be free of fear
when we see him coming to be our Judge,
Jesus Christ, who lives and reigns with you
and the Holy Spirit, one God, now and for ever.
~*Amen.*

READING   *Romans 1:1–4*

Paul, a servant of Jesus Christ, called to be
an apostle, set apart for the gospel of God, which
he promised beforehand through his prophets
in the holy scriptures. the gospel concerning his
Son, who was descended from David according
to the flesh and was declared to be Son of

God with power according to the spirit of
holiness by resurrection from the dead, Jesus
Christ our Lord.

SILENCE

RESPONSE

O gates, lift high your heads, alleluia!
~*Let the king of glory enter! Alleluia!*

CANTICLE OF SIMEON   *Luke 2:29–32*

*All the ends of the earth shall see the salvation
of our God.*

Now, + Lord, you let your servant go in peace:
your word has been fulfilled.

My own eyes have seen the salvation
which you have prepared in the sight of
    every people:

a light to reveal you to the nations
and the glory of your people Israel.

To the Ruler of the ages, immortal, invisible,
the only wise God,
be honor and glory, through Jesus Christ,
for ever and ever. Amen.

INTERCESSIONS

Let us pray to Christ our Savior:
~*O Savior, save us.*

Son of the living God:
~*O Savior, save us.*

Son of David according to the flesh:
~*O Savior, save us.*

Promised One of the holy prophets:
~*O Savior, save us.*

Son of God, according to the spirit of holiness:
~*O Savior, save us.*

By the prayers of your blessed Mother and of all the saints:
~*O Savior, save us.*

LORD'S PRAYER

CLOSING PRAYER

Almighty and merciful God,
by the birth of your only-begotten Son,
set us free from the bondage of sin
and bring us into the land of peace and plenty,
through the same Christ our Lord.
~*Amen.*

May Jesus, the light and life of the world,
+ bless us and keep us.
~*Amen.*

AN EVENING ANTHEM TO MARY DURING THE CHRISTMAS SEASON

Mary of Bethlehem,
crowned with heaven's glory,
look on us, Mother, as we sing your praises.
Be with us always, joy of saints and angels,
joy of creation.

Come to Christ's cave, all who serve our Lady:
sing to God's glory, young and old together,
full hearts outpouring Mary's song of worship,
thanking her Maker.

Sing to the Father, who exalts his handmaid;
sing to God's wisdom, Son who chose his
   Mother;
sing to their Spirit, Love that overshadowed
Mary, chaste Virgin.

The Word was made flesh, alleluia!
~*And dwelt among us, alleluia!*

Father everlasting,
you have established in the Virgin Mary

the royal throne of your wisdom.
Enlighten the church by the Word of life,
that we may walk in the splendor of truth
and come to the full knowledge of your
   mystery of love.
Grant this through our Lord Jesus Christ,
   your Son,
who lives and reigns with you
   and the Holy Spirit,
one God, for ever and ever.
~*Amen.*

May the divine assistance **+** remain always
with us.
~*Amen.*

DECEMBER 25
CHRISTMAS
MORNING

O Lord, **+** open my lips.
~*And my mouth shall declare your praise.*

Glory to God in the highest.
~*And peace to God's people on earth.*

HYMN

PSALM 96

The Lord is coming, and in the morning you will see God's glory.

O sing a new song to the LORD,
sing to the LORD all the earth.
O sing to the LORD, bless his name.

Proclaim God's help day by day,
tell among the nations his glory
and his wonders among all the peoples.

The LORD is great and worthy of praise,
to be feared above all gods;
the gods of the heathens are naught.

It was the LORD who made the heavens.
His are majesty and honor and power
and splendor in the holy place.

Give the LORD, you families of peoples,
give the LORD glory and power;
give the LORD the glory of his name.

Bring an offering and enter God's courts,
worship the LORD in the temple.
O earth, stand in fear of the LORD.

Proclaim to the nations: "God is king."
The world was made firm in its place;
God will judge the people in fairness.

Let the heavens rejoice and earth be glad,
let the sea and all within it thunder praise,
let the land and all it bears rejoice,
all the trees of the wood shout for joy

at the presence of the LORD who comes,
who comes to rule the earth,
comes with justice to rule the world,
and to judge the peoples with truth.

PSALM PRAYER

At the coming in the flesh
of your own dear Son,
O great Judge of all nations,
help us to sing the new song
of your loving presence
as we see your majesty, honor and power
in the face of our blessed Savior.
We ask this in Jesus' name.
~*Amen.*

READING   *Luke 2:15–18*

When the angels had left them and gone into
heaven, the shepherds said to one another,
"Let us go now to Bethlehem and see this thing
that has taken place, which the Lord has made
known to us." So they went with haste and
found Mary and Joseph, and the child lying in

the manger. When they saw this, they made known what had been told them about this child; and all who heard it were amazed at what the shepherds told them.

SILENCE

RESPONSE

Mary treasured all these words, alleluia!
~*And pondered them in her heart, alleluia!*

CANTICLE OF THE HEAVENLY HOST

Glory to God in the highest,
and peace to God's people on earth.

Lord God, heavenly King,
almighty God and Father,
we worship you, we give you thanks,
we praise you for your glory.

Lord Jesus Christ, only Son of the Father,
Lord God, Lamb of God,
you take away the sin of the world:
have mercy on us;
you are seated at the right hand of the Father:
receive our prayer.

For you alone are the Holy One.
you alone are the Lord,
you alone are the Most High.
Jesus Christ,
with the Holy Spirit,
in the glory of God the Father. Amen.

LORD'S PRAYER

CLOSING PRAYER

Almighty God and Father of light,
your eternal Word leaped down from heaven
in the silent watches of the night,
and now your church is filled with wonder
at the nearness of her God.
Open our hearts to receive his life
that our lives may be filled with his peace,
who lives and reigns for ever and ever.
~*Amen.*

May the Word made flesh, full of grace and
truth, **+** bless us and keep us.
~*Amen.*

Light and peace **+** in Jesus Christ our Lord.
~Thanks be to God.

All the ends of the earth have seen, alleluia!
~The salvation of our God, alleluia!

HYMN

PSALM 97

*I bring you good news of great joy: A Savior is
born for you today.*

The LORD is king, let earth rejoice,
let all the coastlands be glad.
Surrounded by cloud and darkness;
justice and right, God's throne.

A fire prepares the way;
it burns up foes on every side.
God's lightnings light up the world,
the earth trembles at the sight.

The mountains melt like wax
before the LORD of all the earth.
The skies proclaim God's justice;
all peoples see God's glory.

Let those who serve idols be ashamed,
those who boast of their worthless gods.
All you spirits, worship the Lord.

Zion hears and is glad;
the people of Judah rejoice
because of your judgments, O LORD.

For you indeed are the LORD
most high above all the earth,
exalted far above all spirits.

The LORD loves those who hate evil,
guards the souls of the saints,
and sets them free from the wicked.

Light shines forth for the just
and joy for the upright of heart.
Rejoice, you just, in the LORD;
give glory to God's holy name.

PSALM PRAYER

Lord Jesus Christ,
your birth is the joy of the whole world
as you come to do the will of God who sent you.
Quench our thirst for things eternal
with fresh streams of your life-giving Spirit;
for yours is the power and the glory,
now and for ever.
~*Amen.*

READING   *Titus 3:4–7*

When the goodness and loving kindness of God
our Savior appeared, he saved us, not because
of any works of righteousness that we had done,
but according to his mercy, through the water
of rebirth and renewal by the Holy Spirit.
This Spirit he poured out on us richly through
Jesus Christ our Savior, so that, having been
justified by his grace, we might become heirs
according to the hope of eternal life.

SILENCE

RESPONSE

The Word was made flesh, alleluia, alleluia!
~*And dwelt among us, alleluia, alleluia!*

THE CANTICLE OF MARY   *Luke 1:46–55*

*Today Christ is born; today the Savior has
appeared; today the angels are singing on earth
and the archangels are rejoicing; today the saints
exult and say: Glory to God in the highest,
alleluia!*

My soul **+** proclaims the greatness of the Lord,
my spirit rejoices in God my Savior,
for you, Lord, have looked with favor on your
    lowly servant.

From this day all generations will call me
    blessed:
you, the Almighty, have done great things for me
and holy is your name.
You have mercy on those who fear you,
from generation to generation.

You have shown strength with your arm
and scattered the proud in their conceit,
casting down the mighty from their thrones
and lifting up the lowly.
You have filled the hungry with good things
and sent the rich away empty.

You have come to the aid of your servant Israel,
to remember the promise of mercy,
the promise made to our forebears,
to Abraham and his children for ever.

Glory to the Father, and to the Son,
and to the Holy Spirit:
as it was in the beginning, is now,
and will be for ever. Amen.

INTERCESSIONS

You, Christ, are the king of glory:
~*The eternal Son of the Father.*

When you took our flesh to set us free:
~*You humbly chose the Virgin's womb.*

You overcame the sting of death:
~And opened the kingdom of God to all believers.

You are seated at God's right hand in glory:
~We believe that you will come to be our judge.

Come, then, Lord and help your people:
~Bought with the price of your own blood.

And bring us with your saints:
~To glory everlasting.

LORD'S PRAYER

CLOSING PRAYER

Abba, dear Father,
we praise you for creating us
in your own image and likeness
and even more for restoring us
in Christ, your living Word.
As we rejoice in his birth,
may we live his gospel,
through the same Christ our Lord.
~Amen.

May the birth of our God and Savior Jesus
Christ **+** bring all humanity to salvation.
~Amen.

AN EVENING ANTHEM TO MARY DURING CHRISTMAS, *page 79*

Morning and Evening Prayer for December 25 is used during the octave of Christmas, through December 31. The following closing prayer may be used as an alternative:

ALTERNATIVE CLOSING PRAYER

Almighty and everlasting God,
by your tender love toward humankind,
you sent your Son, our Savior Jesus Christ,
to take our flesh and set us free.
In your loving-kindness
may we follow the example of his humility
and be made sharers in his noble resurrection,
through the same Christ our Lord.
~Amen.

JANUARY 1
MARY, THE MOTHER OF GOD
MORNING

O Lord, + open my lips.
~And my mouth shall declare your praise.

The child to whom you gave birth, O Mary.
~Is the Ruler of heaven and earth.

HYMN

PSALM 45

You are my Son. It is I who have begotten you this day.

My heart overflows with noble words.
To the king I must speak the song I have made,
my tongue as nimble as the pen of a scribe.

You are the fairest of the men on earth
and graciousness is poured upon your lips,
because God has blessed you for evermore.

O mighty one, gird your sword upon
    your thigh;
in splendor and state, ride on in triumph
for the cause of truth and goodness and right.

Take aim with your bow in your dread
    right hand.
Your arrows are sharp, peoples fall beneath you.
The foes of the king fall down and lose heart.

Your throne, O God, shall endure for ever.
A scepter of justice is the scepter of your
    kingdom.
Your love is for justice, your hatred for evil.

Therefore, God your God, has anointed you
with the oil of gladness above other kings;
your robes are fragrant with aloes and myrrh.

From the ivory palace you are greeted
  with music.
The daughters of kings are among your
  loved ones.
On your right stands the queen in gold of Ophir.

Listen, O daughter, give ear to my words:
forget your own people and your father's house.
So will the king desire your beauty;
he is your lord, pay homage to him.

And the people of Tyre shall come with gifts,
the richest of the people shall seek your favor.
The daughter of the king is clothed with
  splendor,
her robes embroidered with pearls set in gold.

She is led to the king with her maiden
  companions.
They are escorted amid gladness and joy;
they pass within the palace of the king.

Children shall be yours in place of your
  forebears;
you will make them rulers over all the earth.
May this song make your name for ever
  remembered.
May the peoples praise you from age to age.

PSALM PRAYER

Gracious God,
you wedded your divinity to our humanity
in the incarnation of your dear son, our Savior.
By the intimate cooperation of Jesus and Mary
you engender children from age to age,
who by your loving kindness call you Abba
and rejoice in your love, now and for ever.
~Amen.

READING   *Galatians 4:4–6*

When the fullness of time had come, God sent
his Son, born of a woman, born under the
law, in order to redeem those who were under
the law, so that we might receive adoption as
children. And because you are children, God has
sent the Spirit of his Son into our hearts, crying,
"Abba! Father!" So you are no longer as slave
but a child, and if a child then also an heir,
through God.

SILENCE

RESPONSE

The Word was made flesh, alleluia, alleluia!
~And dwelt among us, alleluia, alleluia!

CANTICLE OF PRAISE TO
OUR MOTHER

We praise you as our Mother,
   we acclaim you as our blessed Lady.
All the earth reveres you,
the daughter of the Eternal One.

The hosts of heaven and all the angelic powers
sing your praise:
the angels join in the dance,
the archangels applaud, the virtues give praise,
the principalities rejoice, the powers exult,
the dominations delight, the thrones make festival,
the cherubim and seraphim cry out unceasingly:

Holy, holy, holy is the great Mother of God,
Mary most holy;
the blessed fruit of your womb
is the glory of heaven and earth.

The glorious choir of apostles,
the noble company of prophets,
the white-robed army of martyrs,
all sing your praise.

The holy church throughout the world
   celebrates you:
the daughter of infinite majesty, the mother of
   God's true and only Son,
the bride of the Spirit of truth and consolation.

You bore Christ, the King of glory,
the eternal Son of the Father.
When he took our nature to set us free,
he did not spurn your virgin womb.
When he overcame death's sting,
he assumed you into heaven.
You now sit with your Son
at God's right hand in glory.
Intercede for us, O Virgin Mary,
when he comes to be our judge.
Help your chosen people
bought with his precious blood.
And bring us with all the saints
into glory everlasting.

Save your people, O holy Virgin,
and bless your inheritance.
Rule them and uphold them,
now and for ever.
Day by day we salute you;
we acclaim you unceasingly.
In your goodness pray for us sinners;
have mercy on us poor sinners.
May your mercy sustain us always,
for we put our trust in you.
In you, dear Mother, do we trust;
defend us now and for ever.

LORD'S PRAYER

CLOSING PRAYER

Father,
source of light in every age,
the virgin conceived and bore your Son
who is called Wonderful God, Prince of Peace.
May her prayer, the gift of a mother's love,
be your people's joy through all ages.
May her response, born of a humble heart,
draw your Spirit to rest on your people.
Grant this through Christ our Lord.
~Amen.

Through the prayers of the Virgin Mother
may the Lord **+** grant us safety and peace.
~Amen.

JANUARY 1
MARY, THE MOTHER OF GOD
EVENING

Jesus Christ **+** is the light of the world.
~A light no darkness can extinguish.

Blessed are you among women, O Mary.
~And blessed is the fruit of your womb, Jesus.

HYMN

PSALM 87

Mary is the city of the Lord Most High.

On the holy mountain is the city
cherished by the LORD.
The LORD prefers the gates of Zion
to all Jacob's dwellings.
Of you are told glorious things,
O city of God!

"Babylon and Egypt I will count
among those who know me;
Philistia, Tyre, Ethiopia,
these will be her children
and Zion shall be called 'Mother'
for all shall be her children."

It is God the Lord Most High,
who gives each a place.
In the register of the peoples God writes:
"These are her children."
and while they dance they will sing:
"In you all find their home."

PSALM PRAYER

Heavenly Father,
your cherished city is the Virgin Mary
whose womb contained the Lord Most High.
May we who call her mother

be her faithful children
and find in her a home for ever.
~*Amen.*

READING *John 1:14–18*

The Word became flesh and lived among us,
and we have seen his glory, the glory as of a
father's only son, full of grace and truth. From
his fullness we have all received, grace upon
grace. The law indeed was given through
Moses; grace and truth came through Jesus
Christ. No one has ever seen God. It is God the
only Son, who is close to the Father's heart,
who has made him known.

SILENCE

RESPONSE

Blessed be the great Mother of God, Mary
most holy, alleluia!
~*Who bore the Savior of the world, alleluia!*

CANTICLE OF MARY *Luke 1:46–55*

*Hail, holy Mother! The child you freely bore is
the maker of heaven and earth, alleluia!*

My soul **+** proclaims the greatness of the Lord,
my spirit rejoices in God my Savior,
for you, Lord, have looked with favor on your
    lowly servant.

From this day all generations will call me
  blessed:
you, the Almighty, have done great things for me
and holy is your name.
You have mercy on those who fear you,
from generation to generation.

You have shown strength with your arm
and scattered the proud in their conceit,
casting down the mighty from their thrones
and lifting up the lowly.
You have filled the hungry with good things
and sent the rich away empty.

You have come to the aid of your servant Israel,
to remember the promise of mercy,
the promise made to our forebears,
to Abraham and his children for ever.

Glory to the holy and undivided Trinity:
now and always and for ever and ever. Amen.

INTERCESSIONS

Lord Jesus Christ, Son of God and Son of Mary
of Nazareth:
~*Hear us and have mercy.*

Lord Jesus Christ, who sent an angel to
announce your coming to Mary:
~*Hear us and have mercy.*

Lord Jesus Christ, who lived in subjection
to Mary and Joseph at Nazareth:
~*Hear us and have mercy.*

Lord Jesus Christ, who saw Mary standing
at the foot of your cross:
~*Hear us and have mercy.*

Lord Jesus Christ, who lifted your Mother
into glory at your right hand:
~*Hear us and have mercy.*

Lord Jesus Christ, who crowned your Mother
as Queen of heaven:
~*Hear us and have mercy.*

Lord Jesus Christ, who willed that your Mother
be praised in every generation:
~*Hear us and have mercy.*

LORD'S PRAYER

CLOSING PRAYER

Almighty and everlasting God,
by the cooperation of the Holy Spirit,
you prepared the Blessed Virgin
to be a worthy dwelling for your Son.
Grant that we who rejoice in her memory
may be freed by her loving prayers
both from present ills and from eternal death,
through the same Christ our Lord.
~*Amen.*

May the heavenly Father who sent his only Son
to manifest himself through Mary
+ bless us and keep us.
~*Amen.*

AN EVENING ANTHEM TO MARY DURING CHRISTMAS, *page 79*

Morning and Evening prayer for January 1, the Solemnity of Mary, the Mother of God, is used on the days that fall between New Year's Day and the celebration of Epiphany.

EPIPHANY OF THE LORD THROUGH BAPTISM OF THE LORD MORNING

O Lord, + open my lips.
~*And my mouth shall declare your praise.*

Come, let us adore Christ with the mystical gifts:
~*Of gold, frankincense, and myrrh, alleluia!*

HYMN

PSALM 98

All the ends of the earth have seen the salvation of our God, alleluia!

Sing a new song to the LORD
who has worked wonders;
whose right hand and holy arm
have brought salvation.

The LORD has made known salvation;
has shown justice to the nations;
has remembered truth and love
for the house of Israel.

All the ends of the earth have seen
the salvation of our God.
Shout to the LORD, all the earth,
ring out your joy.

Sing psalms to the LORD with the harp
with the sound of music.
With trumpets and the sound of the horn
acclaim the King, the LORD.

Let the sea and all within it, thunder;
the world, and all its peoples.
Let the rivers clap their hands
and the hills ring out their joy

at the presence of the LORD, who comes,
who comes to rule the earth.
God will rule the world with justice
and the peoples with fairness.

PSALM PRAYER

Lord God,
let the light of your glory shine within us
and lead us through the darkness of this world
to the radiant joy of our heavenly home.
We ask this through Christ our Lord.
~*Amen.*

READING, EPIPHANY OF THE LORD
Ephesians 3:5–6

In former generations this mystery of Christ
was not made known to humankind, as it has
now been revealed to his holy apostles and
prophets by the Spirit: that is, the Gentiles have
become fellow heirs, members of the same
body, and sharers in the promise in Christ Jesus
through the gospel.

SILENCE

RESPONSE

All the rulers of the earth shall adore him,
alleluia!
~*All the nations shall serve him, alleluia!*

READING, BAPTISM OF THE LORD
Isaiah 61:1–2

> The Spirit of the Lord GOD is upon me,
> because the LORD has anointed me; he has sent
> me to bring good news to the oppressed, to
> bind up the brokenhearted, to proclaim liberty
> to the captives, and release to the prisoners;
> to proclaim the year of the LORD's favor.

SILENCE

RESPONSE

You are my Son, the Beloved, alleluia!
~With you I am well pleased, alleluia!

CANTICLE OF ISAIAH   *Isaiah 60:1–3, 6, 19*

*Today is a holy day adorned with great
mysteries: A star leads the magi to the manger,
water is made wine at the wedding and Christ is
baptized by John in the Jordan, alleluia!*

Arise, shine; for your light has come,
and the glory of the LORD has risen upon you.
For darkness shall cover the earth,
and thick darkness the peoples;
but the LORD will arise upon you,
and his glory will appear over you.
Nations shall come to your light,
and kings to the brightness of your dawn.

A multitude of camels shall cover you,
the young camels of Midian and Ephah;
all those from Sheba shall come.
They shall bring gold and frankincense,
and shall proclaim the praise of the LORD.

The sun shall no longer be your light by day,
nor for brightness shall the moon give light
   to you by night;
but the LORD will be your everlasting light,
and your God will be your glory.

Glory to God: Creator, Redeemer, and Sanctifier,
now and always and for ever and ever. Amen.

LORD'S PRAYER

CLOSING PRAYER FOR EPIPHANY OF THE LORD

Father,
you revealed your Son to the nations
by the guidance of a star.
Lead us to your glory in heaven
by the light of faith.
We ask this through Christ our Lord.
~*Amen.*

CLOSING PRAYER FOR THE BAPTISM OF THE LORD

Lord and Savior,
when you willed to bring to perfection
what you had made from the beginning,
you selected servants to reveal your mysteries:
From the angels, Gabriel;
from humans, the Virgin Mary;
from the heavens, a star;
from the waters, the Jordan River,
by which you washed away the sins
of the world.
Glory to you, O Lord.
~*Amen.*

May the Word made flesh, Son of God and Son
of Mary, + bless us and keep us.
~*Amen.*

EPIPHANY OF THE LORD THROUGH BAPTISM OF THE LORD EVENING

Light and peace + in Jesus Christ our Lord.
~*Thanks be to God.*

Before him all rulers shall fall prostrate.
~*All nations shall serve him.*

HYMN

PSALM 72:1–15, 17

We have seen his star in the East and have come
to adore the Lord.

O God, give your judgment to the king.
to a king's son your justice,
that he may judge your people in justice
and your poor in right judgment.

May the mountains bring forth peace for
   the people
and the hills, justice.
May he defend the poor of the people
and save the children of the needy
(and crush the oppressor).

He shall endure like the sun and the moon
from age to age.
He shall descend like rain on the meadow,
like raindrops on the earth.

In his days justice shall flourish
and peace till the moon fails.
He shall rule from sea to sea,
from the Great River to earth's bounds.

Before him his enemies shall fall,
his foes lick the dusk.
The kings of Tarshish and the seacoasts
shall pay him tribute.

The kings of Sheba and Seba
shall bring him gifts.
Before him all rulers shall fall prostrate,
all nations shall serve him.

For he shall save the poor when they cry
and the needy who are helpless.
He will have pity on the weak
and save the lives of the poor.

From oppression he will rescue their lives,
to him their blood is dear.
They shall pray for him without ceasing
and bless him all the day.

May his name be blessed for ever
and endure like the sun.
Every tribe shall be blessed in him,
all nations bless his name.

PSALM PRAYER

Sovereign God and Father,
you established a reign of justice and peace
for the Son of David, our Lord Jesus Christ.
Extend this reign of justice to every nation

so that true peace may come to all peoples.
Through the same Christ our Lord, we pray.
~*Amen.*

READING, EPIPHANY OF THE LORD
Matthew 2:9–11

The magi set out; and there, ahead of them,
went the star that they had seen at its rising, until
it stopped over the place where the child was.
When they saw that the star had stopped, they
were overwhelmed with joy. On entering the
house, they saw the child with Mary his mother;
and they knelt down and paid him homage.
Then, opening their treasure chests, they offered
him gifts of gold, frankincense, and myrrh.

SILENCE

RESPONSE

They shall bring gold and frankincense, alleluia!
~*And proclaim the praise of the Lord, alleluia!*

READING, BAPTISM OF THE LORD
Mark 1:9–11

In those days Jesus came from Nazareth of
Galilee and was baptized by John in the Jordan.
And just as he was coming up out of the
water, he saw the heavens torn apart and the
Spirit descending like a dove on him. And

a voice came from heaven, "You are my Son, the Beloved; with you I am well pleased."

SILENCE

RESPONSE

I have baptized you with water, alleluia!
~*He will baptize you with the Holy Spirit, alleluia!*

CANTICLE OF MARY   *Luke 1:46–55*

Today the church is united to her heavenly bridegroom. Christ washes away her sins in the Jordan, the magi hasten with gifts to the royal wedding and the guests are gladdened by water made wine, alleluia!

My soul + proclaims the greatness of the Lord,
my spirit rejoices in God my Savior,
for you, Lord, have looked with favor on your
   lowly servant.

From this day all generations will call me
   blessed:
you, the Almighty, have done great things for me
and holy is your name.
You have mercy on those who fear you,
from generation to generation.

You have shown strength with your arm
and scattered the proud in their conceit,
casting down the mighty from their thrones
and lifting up the lowly.
You have filled the hungry with good things
and sent the rich away empty.

You have come to the aid of your servant Israel,
to remember the promise of mercy,
the promise made to our forebears,
to Abraham and his children for ever.

Glory to you, Source of all being,
Eternal Word, and Holy Spirit:
as it was in the beginning, is now,
and will be for ever. Amen.

INTERCESSIONS

By your wondrous birth in time, the timeless
Son of God, we pray:
~*Lord, have mercy.*

By your humble birth, the King of glory
in the cave of Bethlehem, we pray:
~*Lord, have mercy.*

By your splendid manifestation to the
shepherds and the magi, we pray:
~*Lord, have mercy.*

By your lowly submission to Mary and Joseph
of Nazareth, we pray:
~*Lord, have mercy.*

By your holy baptism by John in the Jordan,
we pray:
~*Lord, have mercy.*

By your revealing miracle of the water made
wine at Cana of Galilee, we pray:
~*Lord, have mercy.*

LORD'S PRAYER

CLOSING PRAYER FOR EPIPHANY OF THE LORD

Dear and glorious Father,
by the leading of a star,
you revealed your beloved Son to the Gentiles.
Grant that we who know you now by faith
may be brought to the contemplation
of your majestic and heavenly beauty,
through the same Christ our Lord.
~*Amen.*

CLOSING PRAYER FOR THE BAPTISM OF THE LORD

Almighty, eternal God,
when the Spirit descended on Jesus
at his baptism in the Jordan,
you revealed him as your own beloved Son.

Keep us, your children born of water and Spirit,
faithful to our calling.
We ask this through Christ our Lord.
~*Amen.*

May the Word made flesh, full of grace
and truth, + bless us and keep us.
~*Amen.*

AN EVENING ANTHEM TO MARY DURING CHRISTMAS, *page 79*

Morning and evening prayer for the Epiphany of the Lord and the Baptism of the Lord is used from the solemnity of the Epiphany through the feast of the baptism on the following Sunday. During the interval between the Baptism of the Lord and the Presentation (February 2), you may choose from the offices of the Christmas season.

FEBRUARY 2
PRESENTATION OF THE LORD
MORNING

O Lord, + open my lips.
~*And my mouth shall declare your praise.*

Blessed are you among women, O Mary.
~*And blessed is the fruit of your womb, Jesus.*

HYMN

PSALM 147:12–20

*You are a light to the nations and the glory
of your people Israel!*

O praise the LORD, Jerusalem!
Zion praise your God!

God has strengthened the bars of your gates,
and has blessed the children within you;
has established peace on your borders,
and feeds you with finest wheat.

God sends out word to the earth
and swiftly runs the command.
God showers down snow white as wool,
and scatters hoarfrost like ashes.

God hurls down hailstones like crumbs,
and causes the waters to freeze.
God sends forth a word and it melts them:
at the breath of God's mouth the waters flow.

God makes his word known to Jacob,
to Israel his laws and decrees.
God has not dealt thus with other nations;
has not taught them divine decrees.

PSALM PRAYER

God of mercy and compassion,
you sent forth your Word
to make known your holy will
to the people you have chosen.
Establish peace in your church
and feed us with the finest wheat
of your eucharistic banquet,
through Jesus Christ our Lord.
~*Amen.*

READING   *Malachi 3:1*

See, I am sending my messenger to prepare the
way before me, and the Lord whom you seek
will suddenly come to the temple. Indeed,
the messenger of the covenant in whom you
delight is coming, says the LORD of hosts.

SILENCE

RESPONSE

Mary and Joseph brought the child up
to Jerusalem, alleluia!
~*To present him to the Lord, alleluia!*

CANTICLE OF ZACHARY *Luke 1:68–79*

*Old Simeon took the child in his arms and
praised God, alleluia!*

Blessed are you, + Lord, the God of Israel,
you have come to your people and set them free.
You have raised up for us a mighty Savior,
born of the house of your servant David.

Through your holy prophets, you promised
    of old
to save us from our enemies,
from the hands of all who hate us,
to show mercy to our forebears,
and to remember you're your holy covenant.

This was the oath you swore
    to our father Abraham:
to set us free from the hands of our enemies,
free to worship you without fear,
holy and righteous before you,
all the days of our life.

And you, child, shall be called the prophet
    of the Most High,
for you will go before the Lord to prepare
    the way,
to give God's people knowledge of salvation
by the forgiveness of their sins.

In the tender compassion of our God
the dawn from on high shall break upon us,
to shine on those who dwell in darkness
   and the shadow of death,
and to guide our feet into the way of peace.

Glory to God: Creator, Redeemer, and Sanctifier,
now and always and for ever and ever. Amen.

LORD'S PRAYER

CLOSING PRAYER

Father of Jesus the Messiah,
today your only Son was presented to you
in the temple of your choice.
By his coming in our own flesh and blood,
make us worthy to receive him
in the sacraments of our salvation
and at his coming again in glory.
He lives and reigns with you and the Holy Spirit,
one God, now and for ever.
~*Amen.*

May the Word made flesh, the King of glory,
+ bless us and keep us.
~*Amen.*

FEBRUARY 2
PRESENTATION OF THE LORD
EVENING

Light and peace **+** in Jesus Christ our Lord.
~*Thanks be to God.*

O gates, lift high your head.
~*Let the King of glory enter!*

HYMN

PSALM 48

We ponder your love, O God, within your temple.

The LORD is great and worthy to be praised
in the city of our God,
whose holy mountain rises in beauty,
the joy of all the earth.

Mount Zion, true pole of the earth,
the Great King's city!
God, in the midst of its citadels,
is known to be its stronghold.

For the kings assembled together,
together they advanced.
They saw; at once they were astounded;
dismayed, they fled in fear.

A trembling seized them there,
like the pangs of birth.
By the east wind you have destroyed
the ships of Tarshish.

As we have heard, so we have seen
in the city of our God,
in the city of the LORD of hosts
which God upholds for ever.

God, we ponder your love
within your temple.
Your praise, O God, like your name
reaches the ends of the earth.

With justice your right hand is filled.
Mount Zion rejoices;
the people of Judah rejoice
at the sight of your judgments.

Walk through Zion, walk all round it;
count the number of its towers.
Review all its ramparts,
examine its castles,

that you may tell the next generation
that such is our God,
our God for ever and ever
will always lead us.

PSALM PRAYER

Lord God,
your Son was presented to you
in your earthly temple
and became the temple of your presence.
Make this holy city here below
the shrine of your indwelling presence,
a witness to virtue among the nations.
In Jesus' name.
~*Amen.*

READING   *Luke 2:27–33*

Guided by the Spirit, Simeon came into the temple; and when the parents brought in the child Jesus, to do for him what was customary under the law, Simeon took him in his arms and praised God. And the child's father and mother were amazed at what was being said about him. There was also a prophet, Anna the daughter of Phanuel. At that moment she came, and began to praise God and to speak about the child to all who were looking for the redemption of Jerusalem.

SILENCE

RESPONSE

My eyes have seen the salvation, alleluia!
~*Which you prepared in the sight of every*
people, alleluia!

CANTICLE OF SIMEON   *Luke 2:29-32*

Old Simeon took the child in his arms, alleluia!
But the child was old Simeon's Lord, alleluia!

Now, Lord, + let your servant go in peace:
your word has been fulfilled.

My own eyes have seen the salvation
which you have prepared in the sight
    of every people:
a light to reveal you to the nations
and the glory of your people Israel.

Glory to the Father, and to the Son,
and to the Holy Spirit:
as it was in the beginning, is now,
and will be for ever. Amen.

LORD'S PRAYER

INTERCESSIONS

You, Christ, are the king of glory:
~*The Eternal Son of the Father.*

When you took our flesh to set us free:
~*You humbly chose the Virgin's womb.*

You overcame the sting of death:
~*And opened the kingdom of heaven to all
believers.*

You are seated at God's right hand in glory:
~*We believe that you will come to be our judge.*

Come then, Lord, and help your people:
~*Bought with the price of your own blood.*

And bring us with your saints:
~*To glory everlasting.*

CLOSING PRAYER

Almighty and everlasting God,
old Simeon and Anna the prophetess
rejoiced at the coming of your Son
   into the temple.
May we enter into their joy.
May we await your coming into our lives
and your coming in glory at the end of time.
We ask this through Christ our Lord.
~*Amen.*

By the prayers of the Blessed Virgin Mary
and of Saint Joseph her spouse,
may the Light of the world **+** be our salvation.
~*Amen.*

AN EVENING ANTHEM TO MARY
DURING CHRISTMAS, *page 79*

The Church repeats these words today as she traces the ashen cross upon our foreheads: "Remember, you are dust, and into dust you will return." Thus the Church strikes the opening chord of a symphony that will resound through all the weeks of Lent, until, in the Easter Vigil, it swells to its thrilling climax: "Happy that fault that won so great and glorious a Redeemer." Humbly, then, yet full of confidence, we go to the altar today to receive the ashen cross upon our foreheads. We are humble because we realize our sinful condition, we who must daily fight against the flesh, surrounded all our lives by sorrow, sin, temptation and evil. But we are full of confidence, because all the consequences of original sin are transformed by grace, and in the sign of the Cross and the triumphant power of grace we shall achieve the final victory.

~Pius Parsch, 1884–1954

THE FORTY DAYS OF LENT

FORTY DAYS OF PREPARATION

The season of Lent gradually evolved as a final period of preparation for those to be baptized during the Easter Vigil. Their immersion in the baptismal pool, signing with chrism and the cross, and first eucharist was, and is again today, a dramatic culmination to a long period of fasting, prayer, exorcisms and instructions. Their dying and rising is considered the full enactment of the death and resurrection of Jesus in the midst of the community of believers.

For those already baptized, Lent can be an annual retreat. We recall our own initiation and prepare to renew our baptismal vows during the Easter Vigil, committing ourselves anew to the Christian way of life. Lent is a time of prayer, fasting and almsgiving. It urges us to repent of sin and prepare for the sacrament of penance—that sacrament Saint Jerome called "the second plank of salvation." Through a complete confession of wrongdoing, full repentance with a change of attitude, and a declaration of absolution by a priestly minister, we are reconciled with God and the community. The 40 days of Lent lead to the high holy days of the Triduum and deserve our full attention and devotion. We are asked to give up normal amusements and diversions so that we can concentrate on the central mysteries of our faith—mysteries that will be enacted powerfully in the liturgies of the Triduum.

RECKONING THE TIME

Lent extends from Ash Wednesday to the Mass of the Lord's Supper on Holy Thursday evening. The date of Easter determines the whole paschal cycle. Easter is the first Sunday after the first full moon after the (spring) equinox. Sun and moon and our seven-day week all come into play for the Easter feast. The Triduum begins on Holy Thursday night. We count back 40 days to the First Sunday of Lent and add the 4 days that begin with Ash Wednesday.

O Lord, **+** open my lips.
~And my mouth shall declare your praise.

My sacrifice is a contrite spirit.
~A humbled, contrite spirit you will not spurn.

HYMN

PSALM 95

Worship the Lord in the beauty of holiness.

Come, ring out our joy to the LORD;
hail the rock who saves us.
Let us come before God, giving thanks,
with songs let us hail the Lord.

A mighty God is the LORD,
a great king above all gods,
in whose hands are the depths of the earth;
the heights of the mountains as well.
The sea belongs to God, who made it
and the dry land shaped by his hands.

Come in; let us bow and bend low;
let us kneel before the God who made us
for this is our God and we
the people who belong to his pasture,
the flock that is led by his hand.

O that today you would listen to God's voice!
"Harden not your hearts as at Meribah,
as on that day at Massah in the desert
when your ancestors put me to the test;
when they tried me, though they saw my work.

For forty years I was wearied of these people
and I said: 'Their hearts are astray,
these people do not know my ways.'
Then I took an oath in my anger:
'Never shall they enter my rest.'"

PSALM PRAYER

Rock of our salvation,
Ruler and Creator of all that exists,
may we bow down and worship you,
listening to your voice as you call us
to a change of mind and heart.
In Jesus' name.
~*Amen.*

READING   *Isaiah 58:6–9*

Is not this the fast that I choose: to loose
the bonds of injustice, to undo the thongs of
the yoke, to let the oppressed go free, and
to break every yoke? Is it not to share your
bread with the hungry, and bring the homeless
poor into your house; when you see the
naked, to cover them, and not to hide yourself

from your own kin? Then your light shall break forth like the dawn, and your healing shall spring up quickly. Then you shall call, and the LORD will answer; you shall cry for help, and he will say, Here I am.

SILENCE

RESPONSE

If you offer your food to the hungry:
~*Then your light shall rise in darkness.*

CANTICLE OF ISAIAH   *Isaiah 55:6–11*

Maintain justice, and do what is right, for soon my salvation will come.

Seek the LORD who is still to be found:
call upon God who is yet at hand.
Return to the Lord, who will have compassion:
to our God, who will abundantly pardon.

For my thoughts are not your thoughts:
nor are your ways my ways, says the Lord.
For as the heavens are higher than the earth:
so are my ways higher than your ways
and my thoughts than your thoughts.

For as the rain and the snow come down
   from heaven:
and return not again but water the earth,
causing the earth to bring forth and sprout:
giving seed to the sower and bread
   to the hungry;
so shall my word be that goes forth
   from my mouth:
it shall not return to me empty.
but it shall accomplish that which I desire:
and achieve the purpose for which I sent it.

Glory to God: Creator, Redeemer, and Sanctifier,
now and always and for ever and ever. Amen.

LORD'S PRAYER

CLOSING PRAYER

Almighty God, Father of Jesus Christ,
you call us to a change of heart and mind.
May the Word that proceeds from your mouth
accomplish your purpose in our lives,
making your thoughts our thoughts
and your ways our ways,
through the same Christ our Lord.
~*Amen.*

May the Lord bless + us,
protect us from all evil,
and bring us to everlasting life.
~*Amen.*

Light and peace **+** in Jesus Christ our Lord.
~Thanks be to God.

You, O Lord, are my lamp.
~My God who lightens my darkness.

HYMN

PSALM 1

*Blessed are they who hear the word of God
and keep it.*

Happy indeed are those
who follow not the counsel of the wicked,
nor linger in the way of sinners
nor sit in the company of scorners,
but whose delight is the law of the LORD
and who ponder God's law day and night.

They are like a tree that is planted
beside the flowing waters,
that yields its fruit in due season
and whose leaves shall never fade;
and all that they do shall prosper.
Not so are the wicked, not so!

For they like winnowed chaff
shall be driven away by the wind.
When the wicked are judged they shall not stand,
nor find room among those who are just;
for the LORD guards the way of the just
but the way of the wicked leads to doom.

PSALM PRAYER

Abba, dear Father,
your Son Jesus is our teacher of righteousness.
Make us delight in his way of holiness,
plant us in the flowing waters of our baptism
and let us ponder his gospel by day and by night,
through the same Christ our Lord.
~Amen.

READING   *Joel 2:1, 12–13*

Blow the trumpet in Zion; sound the alarm
on my holy mountain! Let all the inhabitants
of the land tremble, for the day of the LORD
is coming, it is near. Yet even now, says the
LORD, return to me with all your heart, with
fasting, with weeping, and with mourning;
rend your hearts and not your clothing. Return
to the LORD, your God, for he is gracious
and merciful, slow to anger, and abounding in
steadfast love, and relents from punishing.

SILENCE

RESPONSE

Blow the trumpet in Zion; sanctify a fast.
~*Call a solemn assembly; gather the people.*

CANTICLE OF MARY *Luke 1:46–55*

Seek the Lord who is still to be found; call upon God who is yet at hand.

My soul **+** proclaims the greatness of the Lord,
my spirit rejoices in God my Savior,
for you, Lord, have looked with favor on your
    lowly servant.

From this day all generations will call me
    blessed:
you, the Almighty, have done great things for me
and holy is your name.
You have mercy on those who fear you,
from generation to generation.

You have shown strength with your arm
and scattered the proud in their conceit,
casting down the mighty from their thrones
and lifting up the lowly.
You have filled the hungry with good things
and sent the rich away empty.

You have come to the aid of your servant Israel,
to remember the promise of mercy,
the promise made to our forebears,
to Abraham and his children for ever.

Glory to the holy and undivided Trinity:
now and always and for ever and ever. Amen.

INTERCESSIONS

Lord Jesus Christ, grant us pardon and peace:
~*Lord, have mercy.*

Lord Jesus Christ, forgive our sins and neglect:
~*Lord, have mercy.*

Lord Jesus Christ, give us true faith and
undying hope in your love for us:
~*Lord, have mercy.*

Lord Jesus Christ, grant light and peace to the
faithful departed:
~*Lord, have mercy.*

Lord Jesus Christ, unite us in worship with your
Mother Mary and the whole company of heaven:
~*Lord, have mercy.*

LORD'S PRAYER

CLOSING PRAYER

May the incense of our repentant prayer
rise before you, O Lord,
and may your loving-kindness fall upon us,
that with purified minds we may sing your praise
with the whole heavenly host
and glorify you for ever and ever.
~*Amen.*

May the blessing of almighty God,
the Father, the Son, and the Holy Spirit,
✝ descend upon us and remain with us for ever.
~*Amen.*

AN EVENING ANTHEM TO MARY DURING LENT

Hail, Queen of heaven, beyond compare,
to whom the angels homage pay.
Hail, Root of Jesse, Gate of Light,
that opened for the world's new day.

Rejoice, O Virgin unsurpassed,
in whom our ransom was begun.
For all your loving children pray
to Christ, our Savior, and your Son.

Gracious Queen of the universe:
~*Intercede for us with the Lord.*

Abba, merciful Father,
send us your assistance in time of temptation.

May we who celebrate the memory of the holy
    Mother of God
rise from our sins by the help of her intercession.
We ask this through Christ our Lord.
~*Amen.*

May the divine assistance + remain always
with us.
~*Amen.*

*The office of Ash Wednesday is also used on Thursday,
Friday and Saturday morning and on Thursday and
Friday evening of the opening days of Lent.*

SATURDAY EVENING

Jesus Christ + is the light of the world.
~*A light no darkness can extinguish.*

In you is the source of life.
~*And in your light we see light.*

HYMN

PSALM 19:8−15

Your will be done on earth as in heaven.

The law of the LORD is perfect,
it revives the soul.
The rule of the LORD is to be trusted,
it gives wisdom to the simple.

The precepts of the LORD are right,
they gladden the heart.
The command of the LORD is clear,
it gives light to the eyes.

The fear of the LORD is holy,
abiding for ever.
The decrees of the LORD are truth
and all of them just.

They are more to be desired than gold,
than the purest gold
and sweeter are they than honey,
than honey from the comb.

So in them your servant finds instruction;
great reward is in their keeping.
But can we discern all our errors?
From hidden faults acquit us.

From presumption restrain your servant
and let it not rule me.
Then shall I be blameless,
clean from grave sin.

May the spoken words of my mouth,
the thoughts of my heart,
win favor in your sight, O LORD,
my rescuer, my rock!

PSALM PRAYER

Lord and lawgiver,
your guidance is trustworthy
and gladdens our hearts.
Enlighten us with the meaning
of your law
and let us find joy in observing it.
We ask this in Jesus' name.
~*Amen.*

READING   *2 Corinthians 5:17–19*

If anyone is in Christ, there is a new creation:
everything old has passed away; see, everything
has become new! All this is from God, who
reconciled us to himself through Christ, and
has given us the ministry of reconciliation;
that is, in Christ God was reconciling the
world to himself, not counting their trespasses
against them.

SILENCE

RESPONSE

See, now is the acceptable time.
~*See, now is the day of salvation.*

CANTICLE OF MARY   *Luke 1:46–55*

*We urge you not to accept the grace of God
in vain.*

My soul **+** proclaims the greatness of the Lord,
my spirit rejoices in God my Savior,
for you, Lord, have looked with favor on your
    lowly servant.

From this day all generations will call me
    blessed:
you, the Almighty, have done great things for me
and holy is your name.
You have mercy on those who fear you,
from generation to generation.

You have shown strength with your arm
and scattered the proud in their conceit,
casting down the mighty from their thrones
and lifting up the lowly.
You have filled the hungry with good things
and sent the rich away empty.

You have come to the aid of your servant Israel,
to remember the promise of mercy,
the promise made to our forebears,
to Abraham and his children for ever.

Glory to you, Source of all being,
Eternal Word, and Holy Spirit:
as it was in the beginning, is now,
and will be for ever. Amen.

APOSTLES' CREED

INTERCESSIONS

Lord Jesus, make us a new creation:
~*Lord, hear our prayer.*

Lord Jesus, renew our hearts and our minds
according to the pattern of the gospel:
~*Lord, hear our prayer.*

Lord Jesus, remake the world and reconcile it
to God:
~*Lord, hear our prayer.*

Lord Jesus, renew and refresh your church
in the power of the Holy Spirit:
~*Lord, hear our prayer.*

Lord Jesus, grant life and peace to the faithful
departed:
~*Lord, hear our prayer.*

By the prayers of your holy Mother and of
all your saints:
~*Lord, hear our prayer.*

LORD'S PRAYER

Let us pray as Jesus taught us:
~*Our Father . . .*

CLOSING PRAYER

Abba, loving Father,
your Son fasted and prayed forty days,
preparing himself to do your will.
May our Lenten self-denial purge us from sin
and prepare us for a life of testimony and service;
through the same Christ our Lord.
~*Amen.*

May Christ, our Lord and lawgiver,
+ bless us and keep us.
~*Amen.*

AN EVENING ANTHEM TO MARY DURING LENT, *page 134*

SUNDAY MORNING

O Lord, **+** open my lips.
~*And my mouth shall declare your praise.*

Save me, O LORD, in your merciful love.
~*For in death no one remembers you.*

HYMN

PSALM 145:1–13

You are kind and full of compassion, slow to anger and abounding in love.

I will give you glory, O God my king,
I will bless your name for ever.

I will bless you day after day
and praise your name for ever.
You are great, LORD, highly to be praised,
your greatness cannot be measured.

Age to age shall proclaim your works,
shall declare your mighty deeds,
shall speak of your splendor and glory,
tell the tale of your wonderful works.
They will speak of your terrible deeds,
recount your greatness and might.
They will recall your abundant goodness;
age to age shall ring out your justice.

You are kind and full of compassion,
slow to anger, abounding in love.
How good you are, LORD, to all,
compassionate to all your creatures.

All your creatures shall thank you, O LORD,
and your friends shall repeat their blessing.
They shall speak of the glory of your reign
and declare your might, O God,

to make known to all your mighty deeds
and the glorious splendor of your reign.
Yours is an everlasting kingdom;
your rule lasts from age to age.

PSALM PRAYER

Lord God,
merciful friend of humanity,
may we stand before you in purity and holiness
and reverently serve you as Lord and Creator;
yours is the kingdom,
now and for ever.
~*Amen.*

READING *Romans 1:1–4*

Paul, a servant of Jesus Christ, called to
be an apostle, set apart for the gospel of God,
which he promised beforehand through his
prophets in the holy scriptures, the gospel
concerning his Son, who was descended from
David according to the flesh and was declared
to be Son of God with power according to
the spirit of holiness by resurrection from the
dead, Jesus Christ our Lord.

SILENCE

Grace to you and peace from God our Father.
~*And from our Lord Jesus Christ.*

CANTICLE OF ZACHARY *Luke 1:67–7*

I will bless you day after day and praise your
name for ever.

Blessed are you, **+** Lord, the God of Israel,
you have come to your people and set them free.
You have raised up for us a mighty Savior,
born of the house of your servant David.

Through your holy prophets, you promised
of old
to save us from our enemies,
from the hands of all who hate us,
to show mercy to our forebears,
and to remember your holy covenant.

This was the oath you swore
to our father Abraham:
to set us free from the hands of our enemies,
free to worship you without fear,
holy and righteous before you,
all the days of our life.

And you, child, shall be called the prophet
   of the Most High,
for you will go before the Lord to prepare
   the way,
to give God's people knowledge of salvation
by the forgiveness of their sins.

In the tender compassion of our God
the dawn from on high shall break upon us,
to shine on those who dwell in darkness
   and the shadow of death,
and to guide our feet into the way of peace.

Glory to the Father, and to the Son,
and to the Holy Spirit:
as it was in the beginning, is now,
and will be for ever. Amen.

APOSTLES' CREED

LORD'S PRAYER

Let us pray as Jesus taught us:
~*Our Father* . . .

CLOSING PRAYER

Abba, dear Father,
your offer of repentance and forgiveness
stands fast for ever.
May the life, death and rising of your Son

---

be our inspiration and our guide
that we may serve you with pure hearts
and grace the lives of those around us.
We ask this in his blessed name.
~*Amen.*

May the grace of our Lord Jesus Christ,
and the love of God, and the communion
of the Holy Spirit,
+ be with us all, now and for ever.
~*Amen.*

SUNDAY EVENING

Light and peace + in Jesus Christ our Lord.
~*Thanks be to God.*

Light shines forth for the just.
~*And joy for the upright of heart.*

HYMN

PSALM 32

I have come to call not the righteous but sinners.

Happy those whose offense is forgiven,
whose sin is remitted.
O happy those to whom the LORD
imputes no guilt,
in whose spirit is no guile.

I kept it secret and my frame was wasted.
I groaned all day long,
for night and day your hand
was heavy upon me.
Indeed my strength was dried up
as by the summer's heat.

But now I have acknowledged my sins;
my guilt I did not hide.
I said: "I will confess
my offense to the LORD."
And you, Lord, have forgiven
the guilt of my sin.

So let faithful people pray to you
in the time of need.
The floods of water may reach high
but they shall stand secure.
You are my hiding place, O Lord;
you saved me from distress.
(You surround me with cries of deliverance.)

I will instruct you and teach you
the way you should go;
I will give you counsel
with my eye upon you.

Be not like horse and mule, unintelligent,
needing bridle and bit,
else they will not approach you.
Many sorrows have the wicked,
but those who trust in the LORD
are surrounded with loving mercy.

Rejoice, rejoice in the LORD,
exult, you just!
O come, ring out your joy,
all you upright of heart.

PSALM PRAYER

Gracious Father,
your very nature is to pardon and forgive.
Rescue us from our stubborn refusal
to acknowledge our sins,
teach us to confess them in all honesty,
and so possess the joy of being forgiven.
We ask this through Christ our Lord.
~*Amen.*

READING *Deuteronomy 6:4–7*

Hear, O Israel: The LORD is our God, the LORD
alone. You shall love the LORD your God
with all your heart, and with all your soul, and
with all your might. Keep these words that I am
commanding you today in your heart. Recite
them to your children and talk about them when
you are at home and when you are away, when
you lie down and when you rise.

SILENCE

RESPONSE

O come, ring out your joy:
~*All you upright of heart.*

CANTICLE OF MARY *Luke 1:46–55*

Repent and believe in the Good News.

My soul **+** proclaims the greatness of the Lord,
my spirit rejoices in God my Savior,
for you, Lord, have looked with favor on your
    lowly servant.

From this day all generations will call me
    blessed:
you, the Almighty, have done great things for me
and holy is your name.
You have mercy on those who fear you,
from generation to generation.

You have shown strength with your arm
and scattered the proud in their conceit,
casting down the mighty from their thrones
and lifting up the lowly.
You have filled the hungry with good things
and sent the rich away empty.

You have come to the aid of your servant Israel,
to remember the promise of mercy,
the promise made to our forebears,
to Abraham and his children for ever.

Glory to the holy and undivided Trinity:
now and always and for ever and ever. Amen.

INTERCESSIONS

Lord Jesus Christ, teach us to confess our sins:
~Lord, have mercy.

Lord Jesus Christ, grant us pardon and peace:
~Lord, have mercy.

Lord Jesus Christ, give us upright hearts:
~Lord, have mercy.

Lord Jesus Christ, teach us the way to go:
~Lord, have mercy.

Lord Jesus Christ, bind us together in the
communion of saints:
~Lord, have mercy.

CLOSING PRAYER

May our prayers, fasts and almsgiving
be a freewill offering in your sight,
O God of mercy and compassion.
May we rejoice in the gift of forgiveness
and rise to a new life of love and service
in and through our loving Redeemer.
~*Amen.*

May Christ Jesus, Son of God and Son of Mary,
+ be our strength and our guide.
~*Amen.*

AN EVENING ANTHEM TO MARY DURING LENT, *page 134*

MONDAY MORNING

O Lord, + open my lips.
~*And my mouth shall declare your praise.*

From my sins turn away your face.
~*And blot out all my guilt.*

HYMN

PSALM 145:1, 13–21

You are just in all your ways and loving in all your deeds.

I will give you glory, O God my king,
I will bless your name for ever.

You are faithful in all your words
and loving in all your deeds.
You support all those who are falling
and raise up all who are bowed down.

The eyes of all creatures look to you
and you give them their food in due season.
You open wide your hand,
grant the desires of all who live.

You are just in all your ways
and loving in all your deeds.
You are close to all who call you,
who call on you from their hearts.

You grant the desires of those who fear you,
you hear their cry and you save them.
LORD, you protect all who love you;
but the wicked you will utterly destroy.

Let me speak your praise, O LORD,
let all peoples bless your holy name
for ever, for ages unending.

PSALM PRAYER

Abba, dear Father,
faithful and loving in all your ways,
as we recall your mighty deeds on our behalf,

give us new confidence in your care.
In Jesus' name.
~*Amen.*

READING *Isaiah 1:16–17*

Wash yourselves; make yourselves clean;
remove the evil of your doings from before my
eyes; cease to do evil, learn to do good; seek
justice, rescue the oppressed, defend the
orphan, plead for the widow.

SILENCE

RESPONSE

O wash me more and more from my guilt.
~*And cleanse me from my sin.*

CANTICLE OF ISAIAH
Isaiah 61:1–3, 10, 11

*The Lord will cause righteousness and praise
to spring forth before all the nations.*

The spirit of the Lord God is upon me:
because the Lord has anointed me
to bring good tidings to the afflicted.

The Lord has sent me to bind up the
    broken-hearted:
to proclaim liberty for the captives,
and release for those in prison,
to comfort all who mourn:
to bestow on them a crown of beauty
    instead of ashes,
the oil of gladness instead of mourning:
a garment of splendor for the heavy heart.
They shall be called trees of righteousness:
planted for the glory of the Lord.

Therefore I will greatly rejoice in the Lord:
my soul shall exult in my God,
for God has robed me with salvation
    as a garment:
and clothed me with integrity as a cloak.

For as the earth brings forth its shoots:
and as a garden causes the seeds to spring up,
so the Lord God will cause righteousness
    and praise:
to spring forth before all the nations.

To the Ruler of the ages, immortal, invisible,
the only wise God,
be honor and glory, through Jesus Christ,
for ever and ever. Amen.

LORD'S PRAYER

CLOSING PRAYER

Heavenly Father,
each year you prepare your church for Easter
by the observance of Lent.
Purify the elect for baptism
and lead the baptized to penance.
Teach us self denial and spur us to good deeds.
We ask this through Christ our Lord.
~*Amen.*

May the God of peace + be with all of us.
~*Amen.*

MONDAY EVENING

Jesus Christ + is the light of the world.
~*A light no darkness can extinguish.*

I will walk in the presence of the Lord:
~*In the land of the living.*

HYMN

PSALM 31:1–9, 20, 24

Abba, into your hands I commend my spirit.

In you, O LORD, I take refuge.
Let me never be put to shame.
In your justice, set me free,
hear me and speedily rescue me.

Be a rock of refuge for me,
a mighty stronghold to save me,
for you are my rock, my stronghold.
For your name's sake, lead me and guide me.

Release me from the snares they have hidden
for you are my refuge, Lord.
Into your hands I commend my spirit.
It is you who will redeem me, LORD.

O God of truth, you detest
those who worship false and empty gods.
As for me, I trust in the LORD;
let me be glad and rejoice in your love.

You who have seen my affliction
and taken heed of my soul's distress,
have not handed me over to the enemy,
but set my feet at large.

How great is the goodness of the LORD,
that you keep for those who fear you,
that you show to those who trust you
in the sight of all.

Love the LORD, all you saints.
The LORD guards the faithful
but in turn will repay to the full
those who act with pride.

PSALM PRAYER

Abba, dear Father,
on the cross Jesus placed himself in your care
and surrendered himself completely to your will.
May his trust in you make us confident
of your constant love for us,
through the same Christ our Lord.
~*Amen.*

READING *Romans 5:8–10*

God proves his love for us in that while we
still were sinners Christ died for us. Much more
surely then, now that we have been justified
by his blood, will be saved through him from the
wrath of God. For if while we were enemies,
we were reconciled to God through the death
of his Son, much more surely, having been
reconciled, will we be saved by his life.

SILENCE

RESPONSE

Be strong, let your heart take courage:
~*All who hope in the Lord.*

CANTICLE OF THE MYSTERY OF CHRIST   *1 Timothy 3:16, 6:16*

O praise the Lord, all you nations, acclaim God all you peoples!

Christ Jesus our Lord was manifested
   in the flesh:
and was vindicated in the Spirit;
he was seen by angels:
and proclaimed among the nations;
he was believed on in the world:
and was taken up in glory.

He will be revealed in due time by God:
the blessed and only ruler, the sovereign
   Lord of all,
who alone has immortality:
and dwells in unapproachable light,
whom no one has ever seen or can see:
to whom alone be honor and might for ever
   and ever.

INTERCESSIONS

To the sovereign Lord of all, we pray:
~Lord, have mercy.

For neighborly concern and friendly affection,
we pray:
~Lord, have mercy.

For those who await our care and aid, we pray:
~*Lord, have mercy.*

For the heavily burdened and afflicted, we pray:
~*Lord, have mercy.*

For those who suffer in mind and heart,
we pray:
~*Lord, have mercy.*

For the friendless and abandoned, we pray:
~*Lord, have mercy.*

By the prayers of the Blessed Virgin Mary and
of all the saints, we pray:
~*Lord, have mercy.*

LORD'S PRAYER

CLOSING PRAYER

Heavenly Father,
you have promised to hear the prayers of those
who call to you in the name of Jesus.
Convert our hearts and hands to your designs
that we may work and pray for the world's
    salvation;
through the same Christ our Lord.
~*Amen.*

May the Lord **+** bless us and take care of us.
May the Lord **+** be kind and gracious to us.
May the Lord look on us with favor
and **+** give us peace.
~Amen.

AN EVENING ANTHEM TO MARY DURING LENT, *page 134*

TUESDAY MORNING

O Lord, **+** open my lips.
~And my mouth shall declare your praise.

Have mercy on me, God, in your kindness.
In your compassion blot out my offense.

HYMN

PSALM 146

It is the Lord who keeps faith for ever.

My soul, give praise to the LORD;
I will praise the LORD all my days,
make music to my God while I live.

Put no trust in the powerful,
mere mortals in whom there is no help.
Take their breath, they return to clay
and their plans that day come to nothing.

They are happy who are helped by Jacob's God,
whose hope is in the LORD their God,
who alone made heaven and earth,
the seas and all they contain.

It is the Lord who keeps faith for ever,
who is just to those who are oppressed.
It is God who gives bread to the hungry,
the LORD, who set's prisoners free,

the LORD who gives sight to the blind,
who raises up those who are bowed down,
the LORD, who protects the stranger
and upholds the widow and orphan.

It is the LORD who loves the just
but thwarts the path of the wicked.
The LORD will reign for ever,
Zion's God, from age to age.

PSALM PRAYER

Faithful God,
the hope of those who trust in you,
rescue the troubled and afflicted,
set us free from our sins

and preserve us in your truth,
through Christ our Lord.
~*Amen.*

READING *Isaiah 1:18–20*

Come now, let us argue it out, says the LORD:
though your sins are like scarlet, they shall be
like snow; though they are red like crimson,
they shall become like wool. If you are willing
and obedient, you shall eat the good of the
land; but if you refuse and rebel, you shall be
devoured by the sword; for the mouth of the
LORD has spoken.

SILENCE

RESPONSE

Come let us walk:
~*In the light of the Lord.*

CANTICLE OF KING DAVID
1 Chronicles 29:10–13

You, O Lord, are exalted as head above all.

Blessed are you, O LORD, the God
of our ancestor Israel, forever and ever.
Yours, O LORD, are the greatness, the power,
the glory, the victory, and the majesty;

for all that is in the heaven
and on the earth is yours;
yours is the kingdom, O Lord,
and you are exalted as head above all.

Riches and honor come from you,
and you rule over all.
In your hand are power and might;
and it is in your hand to make great
and to give strength to all.

And now, our God, we give thanks to you
and praise your glorious name.

LORD'S PRAYER

CLOSING PRAYER

Heavenly Father,
guard us from within and from without,
that we who cannot rely on our own strength
may be protected from all bodily harm
and cleansed of all evil thoughts,
through Jesus Christ our Lord.
~*Amen.*

May the grace of our Lord Jesus Christ
+ be with our spirit.
~*Amen.*

TUESDAY EVENING

Light and peace **+** in Jesus Christ our Lord.
~Thanks be to God.

Your word is a lamp for my feet.
~And a light for my path.

HYMN

PSALM 33:1–21

May your love be upon us, O Lord, as we place
all our hope in you.

Ring out your joy to the LORD, O you just;
for praise is fitting for loyal hearts.

Give thanks to the LORD upon the harp,
with a ten-stringed lute play your songs.
Sing to the Lord a song that is new,
play loudly, with all your skill.

For the word of the LORD is faithful
and all his works done in truth.
The LORD loves justice and right
and fills the earth with love.

By God's word the heavens were made,
by the breath of his mouth all the stars.
God collects the waves of the ocean;
and stores up the depths of the sea.

Let all the earth fear the LORD,
all who live in the world stand in awe.
For God spoke; it came to be.
God commanded; it sprang into being.

The LORD foils the designs of the nations,
and defeats the plans of the peoples.
The counsel of the LORD stands forever,
the plans of God's heart from age to age.

They are happy whose God is the LORD,
the people who are chosen as his own.
From the heavens the LORD looks forth
and sees all the peoples of the earth.

From the heavenly dwelling God gazes
on all the dwellers on the earth;
God who shapes the hearts of them all
and considers all their deeds.

A king is not saved by his army,
nor a warrior preserved by his strength.
A vain hope for safety is the horse;
despite its power it cannot save.

The LORD looks on those who fear him,
on those who hope in his love,
to rescue their souls from death,
to keep them alive in famine.

Our soul is waiting for the LORD.
The Lord is our help and our shield.
Our hearts find joy in the Lord.
We trust in God's holy name.

PSALM PRAYER

Creator and redeemer of the world,
your great plan, your eternal purpose
is to bring the whole universe back to you
through the Word made flesh.
Make us that happy people
who cooperate in carrying out your will,
who bear witness to your constant love.
We ask this through the same Christ our Lord.
~*Amen.*

READING   *1 Corinthians 1:26–30*

Consider your own call, brothers and sisters:
not many of you were wise by human stan-
dards, not many were powerful, not many were
of noble birth. But God chose what is foolish
in the world to shame the wise; God chose what
is weak in the world to shame the strong; God
chose what is low and despised in the world,
things that are not, to reduce to nothing things
that are, so that no one might boast in the
presence of God. He is the source of your life

in Christ Jesus, who became for us wisdom
from God, and righteousness and sanctification
and redemption.

SILENCE

RESPONSE

I decided to know nothing among you:
~*Except Jesus Christ, and him crucified.*

CANTICLE OF SAINT JOHN THE DIVINE   *Revelation 15:3 – 4, 5:13*

*Holy is God, + holy and strong, holy and living
for ever.*

Great and amazing are your deeds,
LORD God the almighty!
Just and true are your ways,
King of the nations.

Lord, who will not fear and glorify your name?
For you alone are holy.

All nations will come and worship before you,
for your judgments have been revealed.

To the One seated on the throne and
    to the Lamb
be blessing and honor and glory and might
forever and ever! Amen.

INTERCESSIONS

For grace, mercy and peace from on high,
we pray:
~*Lord, have mercy.*

For the destruction of all demonic powers,
we pray:
~*Lord, have mercy.*

For those who serve the needs and defend the
rights of all people, we pray:
~*Lord, have mercy.*

For peace and good will among states and
nations, we pray:
~*Lord, have mercy.*

For the elimination of slavery, exploitation and
war, we pray:
~*Lord, have mercy.*

For peace and rest for the faithful departed,
we pray:
~*Lord, have mercy.*

LORD'S PRAYER

CLOSING PRAYER

Almighty and everlasting God,
you want to establish justice and peace
in our hearts and in our nations.
Help us to discover your divine purposes

and to work for the coming of your reign,
through Jesus Christ our Lord.
~*Amen.*

Grace **+** be with us all who have an undying
love for our Lord Jesus Christ.
~*Amen.*

AN EVENING ANTHEM TO MARY DURING LENT, *page 134*

WEDNESDAY MORNING

O Lord, **+** open my lips.
~*And my mouth shall declare your praise.*

From my sins turn away your face.
~*And blot out all my guilt.*

HYMN

PSALM 147

The Lord delights in those who revere him.

Sing praise to the LORD who is good;
sing to our God who is loving:
to God our praise is due.

The LORD builds up Jerusalem
and brings back Israel's exiles,
God heals the broken-hearted,
and binds up all their wounds.
God fixes the number of the stars;
and calls each one by its name.

Our Lord is great and almighty;
God's wisdom can never be measured.
The LORD raises the lowly;
and humbles the wicked to the dust.
O sing to the LORD, giving thanks;
sing psalms to our God with the harp.

God covers the heavens with clouds,
and prepares the rain for the earth;
making mountains sprout with grass
and with plants to serve our needs.
God provides the beasts with their food
and the young ravens when they cry.

God takes no delight in horses' power
nor pleasure in warriors' strength.
The LORD delights in those who revere him,
to those who wait for his love.

PSALM PRAYER

Abba, dear Father,
build up your church,
feed it with the bread of truth

and mend its separations,
that we might truly manifest
one holy, catholic and apostolic church.
For Christ's sake.
~*Amen.*

READING   *Jeremiah 17:7–8*

Blessed are those who trust in the LORD, whose
trust is the LORD. They shall be like a tree
planted by water, sending out its roots by the
stream. It shall not fear when heat comes,
and its leaves shall stay green; in the year of
drought it is not anxious, and it does not cease
to bear fruit.

SILENCE

RESPONSE

All who forsake you, O Lord, shall be put
to shame.
~*For they have forsaken the fountain of
living water.*

CANTICLE OF THE THREE YOUTHS
Daniel 3:52–57

Blest be God's holy and wonderful name!

Blest are you, God of our ancestors,
praised and glorified above all for ever!
Blest be your holy and wonderful name,
praised and glorified above all for ever!

Blest are you in your temple of glory,
praised and glorified above all for ever!
Blest are you enthroned on the cherubim,
praised and glorified above all for ever!

Blest are you who look into the depths,
praised and glorified above all for ever!
Blest are you above the vault of heaven,
praised and glorified above all for ever!

Bless the Lord, sing to God's glory,
all things fashioned by God's mighty hand.
Bless the Father, the Son, and the Holy Spirit,
praised and glorified above all for ever!

LORD'S PRAYER

CLOSING PRAYER

Abba, dear Father,
hear the prayers of your faithful people
and come to their assistance today,
that we may know, love and serve you in this life
and be happy with you for ever in the next.
We ask this through Christ our Lord.
~*Amen.*

May peace **+** be to the whole community,
and love with faith, from God the Father
and the Lord Jesus Christ.
~Amen.

WEDNESDAY EVENING

Jesus Christ **+** is the light of the world.
~A light no darkness can extinguish.

I will prepare a lamp for my Anointed.
~On him my crown shall shine.

HYMN

PSALM 130

*My soul is waiting for the Lord. I count on
God's word.*

Out of the depths I cry to you, O LORD,
Lord, hear my voice!
O let your ears be attentive
to the voice of my pleading.

If you, O LORD, should mark our guilt,
Lord, who would survive?
But with you is found forgiveness:
for this we revere you.

My soul is waiting for the LORD.
I count on God's word.
My soul is longing for the Lord
more than those who watch for daybreak.

Because with the LORD there is mercy
and fullness of redemption,
Israel indeed God will redeem
from all its iniquity.

PSALM PRAYER

God of mercy and compassion,
may we who are baptized into the death
of your beloved Son
die to all sin and selfishness
and eagerly await our joyful resurrection,
through the merits of Christ our Savior.
Amen.

READING *Ephesians 4:30–32*

Brothers and sisters: Do not grieve the Holy
Spirit of God, with which you were marked
with a seal for the day of redemption. Put away
from you all bitterness and wrath and anger and
wrangling and slander, together with all malice,
and be kind to one another, tenderhearted,
forgiving one another, as God in Christ has
forgiven you.

SILENCE

RESPONSE

Clothe yourself with the new self:
~*Created according to the likeness of God.*

CANTICLE OF SAINT JOHN THE DIVINE   *Revelation 4:11; 5:9–10, 12*

*By your blood, O Christ, you ransomed us
for God.*

You are worthy, our Lord and God,
to receive glory and honor and power,
for you created all things,
and by your will they existed and were created.

You are worthy, O Christ, to take the scroll
and to open its seals,
for you were slaughtered
and by your blood you ransomed for God
saints from every tribe and language and people
    and nation.

You have made them to be a kingdom
and priests serving our God,
and they will reign on earth.

Worthy is the Lamb who was slaughtered
to receive power and wealth
and wisdom and might
and honor and glory and blessing.

INTERCESSIONS

Lord Jesus, give us true sorrow for our sins:
~*Lord, have mercy.*

Lord Jesus, save us from a sudden and
unprovided death:
~*Lord, have mercy.*

Lord Jesus, deliver us from disease, famine
and war:
~*Lord, have mercy.*

Lord Jesus, guide and protect the Christian
people everywhere:
~*Lord, have mercy.*

Lord Jesus, grant light and peace to those
who have gone before us:
~*Lord, have mercy.*

Through the prayers of the great Mother of
God, Mary most holy, and of the whole
company of heaven:
~*Lord, have mercy.*

LORD'S PRAYER

CLOSING PRAYER

Gracious Father,
we pray to you for your holy catholic church.
Fill it with your truth.
Keep it in your peace.
Where it is corrupt, reform it.
Where it is in error, correct it.
Where it is right, defend it.
Where it is in want, provide for it.
Where it is divided, reunite it;
for the sake of your Son, our Savior Jesus Christ.
~Amen.

The grace of our Lord Jesus Christ **+** be with
our spirit.
~Amen.

AN EVENING ANTHEM TO MARY DURING LENT, *page 134*

THURSDAY MORNING

O Lord, **+** open my lips.
~And my mouth shall declare your praise.

O rescue me, God, my helper.
~And my tongue shall ring out your goodness.

HYMN

PSALM 148

God is the praise of all the saints.

Praise the LORD from the heavens,
praise God in the heights.
Praise God, all you angels,
praise him, all you host.

Praise God, sun and moon,
praise him, shining stars.
Praise God, highest heavens
and the waters above the heavens.

Let them praise the name of the LORD.
The Lord commanded: they were made.
God fixed them forever,
gave a law which shall not pass away.

Praise the LORD from the earth,
sea creatures and all oceans,
fire and hail, snow and mist,
stormy winds that obey God's word;

all mountains and hills,
all fruit trees and cedars,
beasts, wild and tame,
reptiles and birds on the wing;

all earth's nations and peoples,
earth's leaders and rulers;
young men and maidens,
the old together with children.

Let them praise the name of the LORD
who alone is exalted.
The splendor of God's name
reaches beyond heaven and earth.

God exalts the strength of the people,
is the praise of all the saints,
of the sons and daughters of Israel,
of the people to whom he comes close.

PSALM PRAYER

With heavenly hosts and flashing stars,
may all that takes its origin from you
praise and glorify your magnificent name,
Father, Son, and Holy Spirit,
now and for ever.
~*Amen.*

READING   *Romans 6:8–11*

If we have died with Christ, we believe that we
will also live with him. We know that Christ,
being raised from the dead, will never die again;
death no longer has dominion over him. The
death he died, he died to sin, once for all; but

the life he lives, he lives to God. So you also must consider yourselves dead to sin and alive to God in Christ Jesus.

SILENCE

RESPONSE

The wages of sin is death.
~*But the free gift of God is eternal life.*

CANTICLE OF EZEKIEL   *Ezekiel 36:24–28*

I will use you to show the nations that I am holy.

I will take you from every nation and country
and bring you back to your own land.
I will sprinkle clean water on you
and make you clean from all your idols
and everything else that has defiled you.

I will give you a new heart and a new mind.
I will take away your stubborn heart of stone
and give you an obedient heart.

I will put my spirit in you and will see to it
that you follow my laws
and keep all the commands I have given you.

Then you will live in the land I gave your
    ancestors.
You will be my people, and I will be your God.

Glory to the holy and undivided Trinity:
now and always and for ever and ever. Amen.

LORD'S PRAYER

CLOSING PRAYER

Merciful Father,
you are our first beginning and our last end.
Guide and guard our restless and unquiet hearts,
inspire us to love completely
and to serve all with generosity.
In Jesus' name.
~Amen.

May the grace of the Lord Jesus ✛ be with us all.
~Amen.

THURSDAY EVENING

Light and peace ✛ in Jesus Christ our Lord.
~Thanks be to God.

Lift up the light of your face on us, O Lord.
~You alone make me dwell in safety.

HYMN

PSALM 41

*One of you will betray me, one who is eating
with me.*

Happy those who consider the poor and
    the weak.
The LORD will save them in the evil day,
will guard them, give them life, make them
    happy in the land
and will not give them up to the will of
    their foes.
The LORD will give them strength in their pain,
will bring them back from sickness to health.

As for me, I said: "LORD, have mercy on me,
heal my soul for I have sinned against you."
My foes are speaking evil against me.
They want me to die and my name to perish.
They come to visit me and speak empty words,
their hearts full of malice, they spread it abroad.

My enemies whisper together against me.
They all weigh up the evil which is on me.
They say something deadly is fixed upon me
and I will not rise from where I lie.
Thus even my friend, in whom I trusted,
who ate my bread, has turned against me.

But you, O LORD, have mercy on me.
Let me rise once more and I will repay them.
By this I shall know that you are my friend,
if my foes do not shout in triumph over me.
If you uphold me I shall be unharmed
and set in your presence for evermore.

PSALM PRAYER

Lord Jesus,
you experienced our human weakness,
were betrayed by a close disciple.
By your blessed passion and death,
be our comfort and protection
and strengthen us in our weakness.
You live and reign now and for ever.
~*Amen.*

READING *Hebrews 13:12–15*

Jesus suffered outside the city gate in order
to sanctify the people by his own blood. Let us
then go to him outside the camp and bear the
abuse he endured. For here we have no lasting
city, but we are looking for the city that is
to come. Through him, then, let us continually
offer a sacrifice of praise to God, that is, the
fruit of lips that confess his name.

SILENCE

RESPONSE

Come near to God.
~*And God will come near to you.*

CANTICLE OF SAINT PAUL
Colossians 1:15 – 20

> *Christ Jesus is the firstborn of the dead.*

Christ is the image of the invisible God,
the firstborn of all creation.

For in him all things in heaven and on earth
were created, things visible and invisible,
whether thrones or dominions or rulers
   or powers—
all things have been created through him
   and for him.

He himself is before all things,
and in him all things hold together.
He is the head of the body, the church;
he is the beginning, the firstborn from the dead,
so that he might have first place in everything.

For in him all the fullness of God was pleased
   to dwell,
and through him God was pleased to reconcile
to himself all things, whether on earth
   or in heaven,
by making peace through the blood of his cross.

Glory to you, Source of all being,
Eternal Word, and Holy Spirit:
as it was in the beginning, is now,
and will be for ever. Amen.

INTERCESSIONS

From all evil, temptation and sin:
~*Good Lord, deliver us.*

From stubbornness, obstinacy and pride:
~*Good Lord, deliver us.*

From hearts hardened to human need:
~*Good Lord, deliver us.*

From dishonesty, hypocrisy and lying:
~*Good Lord, deliver us.*

From the snares of the enemy and from
everlasting death:
~*Good Lord, deliver us.*

By the prayers of the Blessed Virgin Mary
and of all the saints:
~*Good Lord, deliver us.*

LORD'S PRAYER

CLOSING PRAYER

Grant us, O loving Lord,
in all our ways of life your help,
in all our uncertainties your counsel,

in all our temptations your protection,
in all our sorrows your peace,
for the sake of Christ our Savior.
~Amen.

Peace be **+** to all of us who are in Christ.
~Amen.

AN EVENING ANTHEM TO MARY DURING LENT, *page 134*

FRIDAY MORNING

O Lord, **+** open my lips.
~And my mouth shall declare your praise.

We adore you, O Christ, and we bless you.
~For by your holy cross you have redeemed the world.

HYMN

PSALM 51

God, be merciful to me, a sinner.

Have mercy on me, God, in your kindness.
in your compassion blot out my offense.
O wash me more and more from my guilt
and cleanse me from my sin.

My offenses truly I know them;
my sin is always before me.
Against you, you alone, have I sinned;
what is evil in your sight I have done.

That you may be justified when you
    give sentence
and be without reproach when you judge,
O see, in guilt I was born,
a sinner was I conceived.

Indeed you love truth in the heart;
then in the secret of my heart teach me wisdom.
O purify me, then I shall be clean;
O wash me, I shall be whiter than snow.

Make me hear rejoicing and gladness
that the bones you have crushed may revive.
From my sins turn away your face
and blot out all my guilt.

A pure heart create for me, O God,
put a steadfast spirit within me.
Do not cast me away from your presence,
nor deprive me of your holy spirit.

Give me again the joy of your help;
with a spirit of fervor sustain me,
that I may teach transgressors your ways
and sinners may return to you.

O rescue me, God, my helper,
and my tongue shall ring out your goodness.
O Lord, open my lips
and my mouth shall declare your praise.

For in sacrifice you take no delight,
burnt offerings from me you would refuse;
my sacrifice, a contrite spirit,
a humbled, contrite heart you will not spurn.

PSALM PRAYER

David sinned grievously before you, O God,
but repented at the voice of Nathan the prophet.
We too have sinned against you.
We ask for your forgiveness
and the renewal of our life and commitment.
A humbled, contrite heart you will not spurn.
In Jesus' name we ask it.
~*Amen.*

READING   *Isaiah 53:2-4*

God's servant grew up before him like a young
plant, and like a root out of dry ground; he
had no form of majesty that we should look at
him, nothing in his appearance that we should
desire him. He was despised and rejected by
others; a man of suffering and acquainted with
infirmity; and as one from whom others hide

their faces he was despised, and we held him
of no account.

SILENCE

RESPONSE
All you who pass by, look and see:
~*Is there any sorrow like my sorrow?*

CANTICLE OF MANASSEH
Prayer of Manasseh: 1, 2, 4, 6–7, 11–12, 13–15

My sin, O Lord, is always before me.

O Lord Almighty, God of our ancestors,
you made heaven and earth with all their order.
All things shudder and tremble before
    your power.

Yet immeasurable and unsearchable
is your promised mercy,
for you are the Lord Most High,
of great compassion, long-suffering,
    and very merciful,
and you relent at human suffering.

And now I bend the knee of my heart,
imploring you for your kindness.
I have sinned, O Lord, I have sinned,
and I acknowledge my transgressions.

For you, O Lord, are the God of those
   who repent,
and in me you will manifest your goodness;
for, unworthy as I am, you will save me
according to your great mercy.

I will praise you continually
all the days of my life.
For all the hosts of heaven sings your praise,
and yours is the glory for ever. Amen.

LORD'S PRAYER

CLOSING PRAYER

Almighty and everlasting God,
you willed that our Savior should become
   a man of sorrows
as an example of humility for all.
Grant that we may follow him in suffering
and come to share in his glorious resurrection,
through the same Christ our Lord.
~Amen.

May the glorious passion of our Lord Jesus
Christ **+** bring us to the joys of paradise.
~Amen.

Jesus Christ **+** is the light of the world.
~A light no darkness can extinguish.

You, O Lord, are my lamp:
~My God who lightens my darkness.

HYMN

PSALM 141

Let my prayer arise before you like incense, the
raising of my hands like an evening oblation.

I have called to you, LORD; hasten to help me!
Hear my voice when I cry to you.
Let my prayer arise before you like incense,
the raising of my hands like and evening
    oblation.

Set, O LORD, a guard over my mouth;
keep watch, O Lord, at the door of my lips!
Do not turn my heart to things that are wrong,
to evil deeds with those who are sinners.

Never allow me to share in their feasting.
If the upright strike or reprove me it is kindness;
but let the oil of the wicked not anoint my head.
Let my prayer be ever against their malice.

Their leaders were thrown down by the side
  of the rock;
then they understood that my words were kind.
As a millstone is shattered to pieces on the
  ground,
so their bones were strewn at the mouth
  of the grave.

To you, LORD God, my eyes are turned;
in you I take refuge; spare my soul!
From the trap they have laid for me keep
  me safe;
keep me from the snares of those who do evil.

PSALM PRAYER

Lord Jesus Christ,
in the evening of your life,
with uplifted hands on the cross,
you became an oblation for us all.
By your bitter sufferings
turn our hearts to goodness and truth
and keep us on the path to eternal life,
where you live and reign, now and for ever.
~Amen.

READING   *Mark 10:42–45*

Jesus called his disciples together and said to
them, "You know that among the Gentiles
those whom they recognize as their rulers lord

it over them, and their great ones are tyrants over them. But it is not so among you; but whoever wishes to become great among you must be your servant, and whoever wishes to be first among you must be slave of all. For the Son of Man came not to be served but to serve, and to give his life a ransom for many."

SILENCE

RESPONSE

They have pierced my hands and my feet.
~*I can count every one of my bones.*

CANTICLE OF SAINT PETER
1 Peter 2:21–24

By his wounds we have been healed.

Christ suffered for you,
leaving you an example,
so that you should follow in his steps.

"He committed no sin,
and no deceit was found in his mouth."

When he was abused,
he did not return abuse;
when he suffered,
he did not threaten;
but he entrusted himself
to the One who judges justly.

He himself bore our sins
in his body on the cross,
so that, free from sins,
we might live for righteousness;
by his wounds you have been healed.

Glory to the Father, and to the Son,
and to the Holy Spirit:
as it was in the beginning, is now,
and will be for ever. Amen.

INTERCESSIONS

Christ our Savior, of your own free will,
you accepted the bitter passion for us and for
our salvation:
~*Lord, have mercy.*

Friend of humanity, you embraced the dread
cross and the burial in the tomb:
~*Lord, have mercy.*

You were seen without beauty to give back to
all the splendor of God:
~*Lord, have mercy.*

Like seed you were buried in the ground
and sprang up a hundredfold:
~*Lord, have mercy.*

By your cross you vanquished hell and put dark
death to flight:
~*Lord, have mercy.*

By your piteous death we are delivered from
death and decay:
~*Lord, have mercy.*

By your loving compassion you have redeemed
all the peoples of the earth:
~*Lord, have mercy.*

By the prayers of the Mother of Sorrows and of
all the saints:
~*Lord, have mercy.*

LORD'S PRAYER

CLOSING PRAYER

Lord Jesus Christ, Son of the living God,
set your passion, your cross and your death
between your judgment and our souls.
In your goodness
grant mercy and grace to the living,
forgiveness and rest to the dead;
to the church and to the nations, concord.
You live and reign for ever and ever.
~*Amen.*

May the glorious passion of our Lord Jesus
Christ + bring us to the joys of paradise.
~*Amen.*

AN EVENING ANTHEM TO MARY DURING LENT, *page 134*

SATURDAY MORNING

O Lord, + open my lips.
~*And my mouth shall declare your praise.*

A pure heart create for me, O God.
~*Put a steadfast spirit within me.*

HYMN

PSALM 150

*By the wood of the cross, joy came into the
whole world!*

Praise God in his holy place,
Sing praise in the mighty heavens.
Sing praise for God's powerful deeds,
praise God's surpassing greatness.

Sing praise with sound of trumpet,
Sing praise with lute and harp.
Sing praise with timbrel and dance,
Sing praise with strings and pipes.

Sing praise with resounding cymbals,
Sing praise with clashing of cymbals.
Let everything that lives and that breathes
give praise to the LORD.

PSALM PRAYER

Holy, living and deathless God,
may a harmonious chorus of human praise
blend with the canticles of rejoicing saints,
now and always and for ever and ever.
~*Amen.*

READING *Malachi 1:11*

From the rising of the sun to its setting my
name is great among the nations, and in every
place incense is offered to my name, and a
pure offering; for my name is great among the
nations, says the LORD of hosts.

SILENCE

RESPONSE

My sacrifice is a contrite spirit.
~*A humbled, contrite heart you will not spurn.*

CANTICLE OF AZARIAH
Daniel 3:26–27, 29–30, 34, 42

*O wash me more and more from my guilt and
cleanse me from my sin.*

Blessed are you, O Lord, God of our ancestors,
and worthy of praise;
and glorious is your name forever!

All your works are true
and your ways right,
and all your judgments are true.

We have sinned and broken your law
in turning away from you;
in all matters we have sinned grievously.
We have not obeyed your commandments,
we have not kept them
or done what you have commanded us
for our own good.

For your name's sake
do not give us up forever,
and do not annul your covenant.
Do not put us to shame,
but deal with us in your patience
and in your abundant mercy.

Deliver us in accordance with your marvelous
    works,
and bring glory to your name, O Lord.

To the Ruler of the ages, immortal, invisible,
the only wise God,
be honor and glory, through Jesus Christ,
for ever and ever. Amen.

LORD'S PRAYER

CLOSING PRAYER

Abba, dear Father,
look mercifully on all for whom Christ died,
so that by your grace and protection
they may serve you loyally in your holy church
to the honor and glory of your name,
for the sake of Jesus, our blessed Savior.
~Amen.

May the grace of the Lord Jesus be ✛ with us all.
~Amen.

*Return to page 135 for the second to the fifth weeks
of Lent.*

Our Lord Jesus Christ, having made this day a day of mourning by His death, changed it into a day of rejoicing by His resurrection. Now that we are solemnly commemorating both of these events, let us keep watch in memory of His death, and joyfully welcome His approaching resurrection. This is our annual festival, our Paschal feast. "For Christ our pasch is sacrificed" (1 Corinthians 5:7), and "the old things have passed away; behold, all things are made new" (2 Corinthians 5:17). We mourn because our sins oppress us, and truly rejoice because we are justified by His grace. For, "He was delivered up for our sins, and arose again for our justification" (Romans 4:25). Gladly do we lament our sins while we delight in the Resurrection. And since for our sake He endured sadness as a presage to our gladness, we cannot let the anniversary go by in ungrateful forgetfulness, but rather we should celebrate it in grateful remembrance.

~Saint Augustine of Hippo, 354–430

THE TRIDUUM

In Catholic piety the Triduum is the high point of the Christian year. We prepare by keeping Lent and our celebration overflows to the 50 days of Easter. It was Saint Cyril (315–386), bishop of Jerusalem, who organized the services and processions of the Triduum in and around the holy city. Soon the pilgrims who experienced the celebrations during their visits to the holy sites saw to it that their home churches had similar liturgies.

By celebrating the Three Days, we enter the paschal mystery. We sink into the bitter misery of the betrayed, abandoned, crucified Jesus. We keep vigil around the tomb, listening to the stories of God's saving power. Easter will mean little for us if we do not experience the fasting, vigil and prayer of Good Friday and Holy Saturday. With all our being we enter the paschal mystery: "Dying you destroyed out death . . ." Participating in the liturgies of the Three Days is not a luxury reserved for the pious few; it is radically necessary for a disciple of Jesus crucified, risen and glorified.

RECKONING THE TIME

The Triduum is the turning point between Lent and Easter. Holy Thursday evening we leave Lent to join in the washing of feet and the holy eucharist. Prayer and fasting continue as we celebrate the Lord's Passion and venerate the cross on Good Friday. They extend to the quiet waiting of Holy Saturday until the church assembles in the dark of night to continue the vigil, to baptize, to proclaim the resurrection and to celebrate the eucharist. The Triduum closes with Evening Prayer of Easter Sunday.

Pray these forms of Morning Prayer and Evening Prayer on Holy Thursday evening, on Good Friday and on Holy Saturday.

O Lord, **+** open my lips.
~*And my mouth shall declare your praise.*

We adore you, O Christ, and we bless you.
~*By your cross you have redeemed the world.*

HYMN

PSALM 22:1–22

*They will mock him, spit upon him, flog him,
and kill him; and after three days he will rise.*

My God, my God, why have you forsaken me?
You are far from my plea and the cry of
   my distress.
O my God, I call by day and you give no reply;
I call by night and I find no peace.

Yet you, O God, are holy,
enthroned on the praises of Israel.
In you our forebears put their trust;
they trusted and you set them free.
When they cried to you, they escaped.
In you they trusted and never in vain.

But I am a worm and no man,
the butt of all, the laughing-stock of the people.
All who see me deride me.
They curl their lips, they toss their heads.
"He trusted in the LORD, let him save him,
and release him if this is his friend."

Yes, it was you who took me from the womb,
entrusted me to my mother's breast.
To you I was committed from my birth,
from my mother's womb you have been
   my God.
Do not leave me alone in my distress;
Come close, there is none else to help.

Many bulls have surrounded me,
fierce bulls of Bashan close me in.
Against me they open wide their jaws,
like lions, rending and roaring.

Like water I am poured out,
disjointed are all my bones.
My heart has become like wax,
it is melted within my breast.
Parched as burnt clay is my throat,
my tongue cleaves to my jaws.

Many dogs have surrounded me,
a band of the wicked beset me.
They tear holes in my hands and my feet
and lay me in the dust of death.

I can count every one of my bones.
These people stare at me and gloat;
they divide my clothing among them.
They cast lots for my robe.

O LORD, do not leave me alone,
my strength, make haste to help me!
Rescue my soul from the sword,
my life from the grip of these dogs.
Save my life from the jaws of these lions,
my soul from the horns of these oxen.

PSALM PRAYER

Lord Jesus Christ, suffering servant of God,
you were cruelly betrayed by Judas,
unjustly condemned to death by Pontius Pilate,
mocked, flogged and crowned with thorns,
pierced with nails, scorned by unbelievers
and laid in the dust of death.
By your holy and glorious wounds,
guard us and keep us from all evil
and bring us to the victory you have won for us.
You live and reign now and for ever.
~*Amen.*

READING, GOOD FRIDAY
John 12:23–26

The hour has come for the Son of Man to be glorified. Very truly, I tell you, unless a grain of wheat falls into the earth and dies, it remains just a single grain; but if it dies, it bears much fruit. Those who love their life lose it, and those who hate their life in this world will keep it for eternal life. Whoever serves me must follow me, and where I am, there will my servant be also. Whoever serves me, the Father will honor.

SILENCE

RESPONSE

By a tree we were made slaves.
~*By a cross we were set free.*

READING, HOLY SATURDAY
Hosea 6:1–3

Come, let us return to the LORD; for it is he who has torn, and he will heal us; he has struck down, and he will bind us up. After two days he will revive us; on the third day he will raise us up, that we may live before him. Let us know, let us press on to know the LORD; his appearing is as sure as the dawn; he will come to us like the showers, like the spring rains that water the earth.

SILENCE

RESPONSE

I desire steadfast love and not sacrifice:
~*The knowledge of God rather than burnt offerings.*

CANTICLE OF THE PROPHET ISAIAH
Isaiah 53:1–5

Good Friday:
*Pilate wrote a notice and put it on the cross:
"Jesus of Nazareth, the King of the Jews."*

Holy Saturday:
*Joseph took the body of Jesus, wrapped it in a
clean linen cloth and laid it in his own new tomb.*

Who would have believed what we have heard
and to whom has the power of the Lord been
    revealed?

He grew up before the Lord like a tender plant:
like a root out of arid ground.
He has no beauty, no majesty to draw our eyes:
no grace to make us delight in him.

He was despised and rejected:
a man of sorrows and familiar with suffering.
Like one from whom people hid their faces:
he was despised and we esteemed him not.

Surely he has borne our grief and carried
    our sorrows:
yet we considered him stricken,
smitten by God, and afflicted.
But he was wounded for our transgressions:
he was bruised for our iniquities.
The punishment that brought us peace was
    laid upon him:
and by his wounds we are healed.

To the One seated on the throne and
    to the Lamb,
be blessing and honor and glory and might
for ever and ever!

LORD'S PRAYER

CLOSING PRAYER

Almighty and everlasting God,
you willed that our Savior
should become human like one of us
and undergo the torment of the cross
as an example of humility for all.
Grant that we may follow him in suffering,
share in his glorious resurrection
and live the life of the Spirit,
now and always and for ever and ever.
~*Amen.*

By his holy and glorious wounds,
may Christ Jesus **+** protect us and keep us.
~*Amen.*

HOLY THURSDAY, GOOD FRIDAY AND HOLY SATURDAY EVENING

Jesus Christ **+** is the light of the world.
~*A light no darkness can extinguish.*

We adore you, O Christ, and we bless you.
~*By your cross you have redeemed the world.*

HYMN

PSALM 142

He was wounded for our transgressions and by his bruises we are healed.

With all my voice I cry to you, LORD,
with all my voice I entreat you, LORD.
I pour out my trouble before you;
I tell you all my distress
while my spirit faints within me.
But you, O Lord, know my path.

On the way where I shall walk
they have hidden snare to entrap me.
Look on my right and see:
there is no one who takes my part.
I have no means of escape,
not one who cares for my soul.

I cry to you, O LORD.
I have said: "You are my refuge,
all I have in the land of the living."
Listen, then, to my cry
for I am in the depths of distress.

Rescue me from those who pursue me
for they are stronger than I.
Bring my soul out of this prison
and then I shall praise your name.
Around me the just will assemble
because of your goodness to me.

PSALM PRAYER

Holy Redeemer,
a man of sorrows and acquainted with grief,
you were led to the slaughter like a lamb
but you did not open your mouth against them.
By this suffering, release us from sin
and rouse us from the sleep of death,
O Savior of the world,
living and reigning, now and for ever.
~*Amen.*

READING, HOLY THURSDAY
Hebrews 13:12–16

Jesus suffered outside the city gate in order to sanctify the people by his own blood. Let us then go to him outside the camp and bear the abuse he endured. For here we have no lasting city, but we are looking for the city that is to come. Through him, then, let us continually offer a sacrifice of praise to God, that is, the fruit of lips that confess his name. Do not neglect to do good and to share what you have, for such sacrifices are pleasing to God.

Silence

Response

The cup of salvation I will raise.
~I will call on the Lord's name.

READING, GOOD FRIDAY
Hebrews 2:10–11

It was fitting that God, for whom and through whom all things exist, in bringing many children to glory, should make the pioneer of their salvation perfect through sufferings. For the one who sanctifies and those who are sanctified all have one Father. For this reason Jesus is not ashamed to call them brothers and sisters.

SILENCE

RESPONSE

Look and see, all you who pass by:
~*If there is any sorrow like my sorrow.*

READING, HOLY SATURDAY
Job 19:25, 26b, 27

I know that my Redeemer lives, and that at the
last he will stand upon the earth and then
in my flesh I shall see God, whom I shall see on
my side, and my eyes shall behold, and not
another. My heart faints within me!

SILENCE

RESPONSE

For our sake Jesus became obedient to the point
of death:
~*Even death on a cross.*

CANTICLE OF MARY   *Luke 1:46–55*

Holy Thursday:
*This cup that is poured out for you is the new
covenant in my blood.*

Good Friday:
*Jesus said: "It is finished." Then he bowed his
head and gave up the spirit.*

Holy Saturday:
The women who had come with Jesus from
Galilee saw the tomb and how his body was laid.

My soul **+** proclaims the greatness of the Lord,
my spirit rejoices in God my Savior,
for you, Lord, have looked with favor on your
    lowly servant.

From this day all generations will call me
    blessed:
you, the Almighty, have done great things for me
and holy is your name.
You have mercy on those who fear you,
from generation to generation.

You have shown strength with your arm
and scattered the proud in their conceit,
casting down the mighty from their thrones
and lifting up the lowly.
You have filled the hungry with good things
and sent the rich away empty.

You have come to the aid of your servant Israel,
to remember the promise of mercy,
the promise made to our forebears,
to Abraham and his children for ever.

To the Ruler of the ages, immortal, invisible,
the only wise God,
be honor and glory, through Jesus Christ,
for ever and ever. Amen.

INTERCESSIONS

Lord Jesus, who was betrayed by the kiss of
Judas Iscariot in the Garden of Gethsemane:
~*Hear us and have mercy.*

Lord Jesus, who was condemned to death for us
by Pontius Pilate:
~*Hear us and have mercy.*

Lord Jesus, who was flogged for us at the pillar:
~*Hear us and have mercy.*

Lord Jesus, who was crowned with thorns for
us, mocked and insulted:
~*Hear us and have mercy.*

Lord Jesus, who carried the cross to Golgotha
for us:
~*Hear us and have mercy.*

Lord Jesus, who was crucified for us:
~*Hear us and have mercy.*

Lord Jesus, who was buried for us in the tomb:
~*Hear us and have mercy.*

Lord Jesus, who rose for us on the third day:
~*Hear us and have mercy.*

Lord Jesus, who flooded the world with the
light of the Holy Spirit:
~*Hear us and have mercy.*

CLOSING PRAYER, HOLY THURSDAY AND GOOD FRIDAY

Abba, dear Father,
look upon this family of yours
for which our Lord Jesus Christ
willingly endured the torment of the cross.
He lives and reigns with you and the Holy Spirit,
now and for ever.
~*Amen.*

CLOSING PRAYER, HOLY SATURDAY

Lord Jesus Christ, Son of the living God,
at day's end you rested in the tomb
and made the grave a bed of hope
for those who believe in you.
Life of the world,
when our bodies lie in the dust of death,
may we live with you for ever and ever.
~*Amen.*

By his holy and glorious wounds,
may Christ our Lord + protect us and keep us.
~*Amen.*

What a strange and astonishing situation! We did not really die, we were not really buried, we did not really hang from a cross and rise again. Our imitation was symbolic, but our salvation a reality. Christ truly hung from a cross, was truly buried, and truly rose again. All this he did gratuitously for us, so that we might share his sufferings by imitating them, and gain salvation in actuality. What transcendent kindness! Christ endured nails in his innocent hands and feet, and suffered pain; and by letting me participate in the pain without anguish or sweat, he freely bestows salvation on me. God, who has brought you from death to life, can grant you the power to walk in newness of life (Romans 6:4).

~Saint Cyril of Jerusalem, ca. 313–386

The Fifty days of Easter

FIFTY DAYS OF REJOICING

All high feast days have both a time of preparation
and a time of extension. They are too full of sacred
meaning to be celebrated on a single day. This is especially true of Easter, the unfolding of the new and
eternal covenant, so rich in mystery and symbolism
that we must explore its meaning during a celebration
of 50 days!

Having given our earnest efforts to Lent and
having opened ourselves to the Triduum, we have
sharper vision to behold the triumph of the resurrection. Without Lent and Triduum, the vivid truths of
Easter would be flat and pale.

> Jesus humbled himself
> and became obedient to the point of death—
> even death on a cross.
> Therefore God exalted him
> and gave him the name
> that is above every name.
> —Philippians 2:8–9

During Easter we have a new mission: exuberant
feasting and the compelling work of living into this

mystery, comprehending what our new life in Christ bestows and calls forth in our discipleship.

Morning Prayer and Evening Prayer are an intimate part of this extended celebration, particularly in the home. Let us light our baptismal candles at the home altar and know, as Saint Augustine did, that "we are Easter people and alleluia is our song."

PENTECOST

Pentecost Sunday, the last and fiftieth day of the Easter season, celebrates the outpouring of the Holy Spirit that Jesus had promised before his passion and death (John 14). In the classic account (Acts 2:1–41), Saint Luke describes how the Holy Spirit came in wind and tongues of fire to revitalize and inspire the disciples of Jesus as they waited in the upper room. The remainder of the Acts of the Apostles spells out the results of this wondrous gift, with special emphasis on the missionary careers of the preeminent apostles Peter and Paul.

Whenever and wherever the flame of inspiration and apostleship strikes the church afresh, we can attribute it to the Holy Spirit. In this age of reform and renewal, as we work toward the long-awaited reunion of the churches, we have a special reason to praise and thank the Spirit, our advocate and guide, and to pray: "Come, Holy Spirit, fill the hearts of the faithful and kindle in them the fire of your love."

O Lord, + open my lips.
~*And my mouth shall declare your praise.*

This day was made by the Lord, alleluia!
~*We rejoice and are glad, alleluia!*

HYMN

PSALM 57:1–11

*O God, arise above the heavens; may your glory
shine on earth!*

Have mercy on me, God, have mercy
for in you my soul has taken refuge.
In the shadow of your wings I take refuge
till the storms of destruction pass by.

I call to you God the Most High,
to you who have always been my help.
May you send from heaven and save me
and shame those who assail me.

O God, send your truth and your love.

My soul lies down among lions,
who would devour us, one and all.
Their teeth are spears and arrows,
their tongue a sharpened sword.

O God, arise above the heavens;
may your glory shine on earth!

They laid a snare for my steps,
my soul was bowed down.
They dug a pit in my path
but fell in it themselves.

My heart is ready, O God,
my heart is ready.
I will sing, I will sing your praise.
Awake, my soul;
awake, lyre and harp,
I will awake the dawn.

I will thank you, Lord, among the peoples,
among the nations I will praise you
for your love reaches to the heavens
and your truth to the skies.

Psalm Prayer

Most High God,
you lifted your dear Son from among the dead
and revealed him to the faithful women
    from Galilee
who had followed him even to the hill
    of Golgotha.
Fill our hearts with the joy of the resurrection

and the grace to testify to it in our daily lives.
In Jesus' name we ask it.
~*Amen.*

READING   *Mark 16:1–2, 5–7*

When the sabbath was over, Mary Magdalene,
and Mary the mother of James, and Salome
bought spices, so that they might go and anoint
him. And very early on the first day of the
week, when the sun had risen, they went to the
tomb. As they entered the tomb, they saw a
young man, dressed in a white robe, sitting
on the right side; and they were alarmed. But he
said to them, "Do not be alarmed; you are looking for Jesus of Nazareth, who was crucified.
He has been raised; he is not here. Look, there
is the place they laid him. But go, tell his disciples and Peter that he is going ahead of you
to Galilee; there you will see him, just as he
told you.

SILENCE

RESPONSE

Awake my soul, alleluia!
~*I will awake the dawn, alleluia!*

CANTICLE OF THE CHURCH

We praise you, O God,
we acclaim you as Lord;
all creation worships you,
the Father everlasting.

To you all angels, all the powers of heaven,
the cherubim and seraphim, sing
   in endless praise:
Holy, holy, holy Lord, God of power and might,
heaven and earth are full of your glory.

The glorious company of apostles praise you.
The noble fellowship of prophets praise you.
The white-robed army of martyrs praise you.

Throughout the world the holy Church
   acclaims you:
Father, of majesty unbounded,
your true and only Son, worthy of all praise,
the Holy Spirit, advocate and guide.

You, Christ, are the king of glory,
the eternal Son of the Father.
When you took our flesh to set us free
you humbly chose the Virgin's womb.

You overcame the sting of death
and opened the kingdom of heaven
   to all believers.

You are seated at God's right hand in glory.
We believe that you will come to be our judge.

Come then, Lord, and help your people,
bought with the price of your own blood,
and bring us with your saints
to glory everlasting.

APOSTLES' CREED

LORD'S PRAYER

Let us pray as Jesus taught us:
~*Our Father* . . .

CLOSING PRAYER

Heavenly Father,
when Christ our paschal lamb
shed his blood on the cross
and anointed the door posts of our hearts,
you delivered us from the destroying angel
who passed by our sins for your love.
You led us into the promised land
by pillars of cloud and fire.
Be our rescuing and victorious God again
as all creation dances and sings:
Christ has risen from the dead!
~*Amen.*

Let us bless the Lord, alleluia!
~*Thanks be to God, alleluia!*

May our radiant and dazzling Christ
+ lead us from earth to heaven,
from death to life.
~*Amen.*

SUNDAY EVENING

Light and peace + in Jesus Christ our Lord.
~*Thanks be to God.*

Christ is risen, alleluia!
~*He is risen indeed, alleluia!*

HYMN

PSALM 18:2–11, 17–20, 29, 47, 50–51

*Lord God, you have shown great love for your
Anointed, alleluia!*

I love you, LORD, my strength,
my rock, my fortress, my savior.
God, you are the rock where I take refuge;
my shield, my mighty help, my stronghold.
LORD, you are worthy of all praise,
when I call I am saved from my foes.

The waves of death rose about me;
the torrents of destruction assailed me;
the snares of the grave entangled me;
the traps of death confronted me.

In my anguish I called to you, LORD;
I cried to you, God, for help.
From your temple you heard my voice;
my cry came to your ears.

Then the earth reeled and rocked;
the mountains were shaken to their base,
they reeled at your terrible anger.
Smoke came from your nostrils
and scorching fire from your mouth,
coals were set ablaze by its heat.

You lowered the heavens and came down,
a black cloud under your feet.
You came enthroned on the cherubim,
you flew on the wings of the wind.

From on high you reached down and seized me;
you drew me out of mighty waters.
You snatched me from my powerful foe,
from my enemies whose strength I could
    not match.

They assailed me in the day of my misfortune,
but you, LORD, were my support.
You brought me forth into freedom,
you saved me because you loved me.

You, O LORD, are my lamp,
my God who lightens my darkness.
With you I can break through any barrier,
with my God I can scale any wall.

Long life to you, LORD, my rock!
Praise to you, God, who saves me,
the God who gives me redress
and subdues people under me.

I will praise you, LORD, among the nations;
I will sing a psalm to your name.

You have given great victories to your king
and shown your love for your anointed.

PSALM PRAYER

Lord of life,
by the mighty resurrection of your Son,
you have delivered us from sin and death
and made us a new creation.
By the power of his rising,
give us a life that is stronger than death
that we may serve you and one another
through time and eternity.
In Jesus' name.
~*Amen.*

READING   *John 3:14–17*

Just as Moses lifted up the serpent in the
wilderness, so must the Son of Man be lifted up,
that whoever believes in him may have eternal
life. For God so loved the world that he gave
his only Son, so that everyone who believes in
him may not perish but may have eternal life.
Indeed, God did not send the Son into the
world to condemn the world, but in order that
the world might be saved through him.

SILENCE

RESPONSE

We adore your cross, O Lord, alleluia!
*~And we praise and glorify your holy
resurrection, alleluia!*

CANTICLE FOR EASTER
*1 Corinthians 5:7–8; Romans 6:9–11;
1 Corinthians 15:20–21*

> *Alleluia, alleluia, alleluia!*

Christ our Passover has been sacrificed for us;
Therefore let us keep the feast,
Not with the old leaven, the leaven of malice
    and evil,
but with the unleavened bread of sincerity
    and truth. Alleluia.

Christ being raised from the dead will
  never die again;
death no longer has dominion over him.
The death he died, he died to sin, once for all;
but the life he lives, he lives to God.
So also consider yourselves dead to sin,
and alive to God in Jesus Christ our Lord.
  Alleluia.

Christ has been raised from the dead,
the first fruits of those who have fallen asleep.
For since by a man came death,
by a man has come also the resurrection of
  the dead.
For as in Adam all die,
so also in Christ shall all be made alive. Alleluia.

Glory to the Father, and to the Son,
and to the Holy Spirit:
as it was in the beginning, is now,
and will be for ever. Amen.

INTERCESSIONS

Lord Jesus, who died for ours sins and rose
for our resurrection:
~*Grant us peace.*

Lord Jesus, who trampled down death by
your death:
~*Grant us peace.*

Lord Jesus, who brought life to those in
the grave:
~*Grant us peace.*

Lord Jesus, who overcame death's sting
and gave fresh life to a fallen world:
~*Grant us peace.*

Lord Jesus, our new life and our resurrection
from the dead:
~*Grant us peace.*

By the prayers of the great Mother of God,
Mary most holy and of all the saints:
~*Grant us peace.*

LORD'S PRAYER

CLOSING PRAYER

Abba, dear Father,
in virtue of our baptism,
by which we are buried with Christ in death
and raised to new life in the Spirit,
absolve us from all our sins
and bring us to the full enjoyment
of the indwelling Holy Spirit.
We ask this through the new Adam,
Jesus Christ, your Son.
~*Amen.*

Let us bless the Lord, alleluia!
~*Thanks be to God, alleluia!*

May the grace of our Lord Jesus Christ,
and the love of God, and the communion of the
Holy Spirit, + remain with us for ever.
~*Amen.*

AN EVENING ANTHEM TO MARY DURING EASTER

Rejoice, O Queen of heaven, alleluia!
for the Son you bore, alleluia!
has arisen as he promised, alleluia!
Pray for us to God the Father, alleluia!

Rejoice and be glad, O Virgin Mary, alleluia!
~*For the Lord has truly risen, alleluia!*

Holy, immortal and living God,
joy came into the world
when you lifted your dear Son
from among the dead.
By the prayers of Mary his Mother,
and of all the myrrh-bearing women,
raise us with Jesus
and bring us to the happiness of everlasting life,
through the same Christ our Lord.
~*Amen.*

By the power of Christ's resurrection
and the prayers of the whole company of heaven,
may God + grant us safety and peace.
~*Amen.*

O Lord, **+** open my lips.
~*And my mouth shall declare your praise.*

O Lord, you search me and you know me,
alleluia!
~*You know my resting and my rising, alleluia!*

HYMN

PSALM 139:1–18, 23–24

God lifted Jesus high and gave him the name
above all other names, alleluia!

O Lord, you search me and you know me,
you know my resting and my rising,
you discern my purpose from afar.
You mark when I walk or lie down,
all my ways lie open to you.

Before ever a word is on my tongue
you know it, O LORD, through and through.
Behind and before you besiege me,
your hand ever laid upon me.
Too wonderful for me, this knowledge,
too high, beyond my reach.

O where can I go from your spirit,
or where can I flee from your face?
If I climb the heavens, you are there.
If I lie in the grave, you are there.

If I take the wings of the dawn
and dwell at the sea's furthest end,
even there your hand would lead me,
your right hand would hold me fast.

If I say, "Let the darkness hide me
and the light around me be night,"
even darkness is not dark for you
and the night is as clear as the day.

For it was you who created my being,
knit me together in my mother's womb.
I thank you for the wonder of my being,
for the wonders of all your creation.

Already you knew my soul,
my body held no secret from you
when I was being fashioned in secret
and molded in the depths of the earth.

Your eyes saw all my actions,
they were all of them written in your book;
every one of my days was decreed
before one of them came into being.

To me, how mysterious your thoughts,
the sum of them not to be numbered!
If I count them, they are more than the sand;
to finish, I must be eternal like you.

O search me, God, and know my heart.
O test me and know my thoughts.
See that I follow not the wrong path
and lead me in the path of life eternal.

PSALM PRAYER

Abba, dear Father,
your beloved Son went down among the dead
to bring them the Good News
and rose again in glory on the third day.
In your kindness,
help us to commit ourselves anew
to the vows of our baptism
and so enjoy the happiness of the redeemed.
We ask this in the name of Jesus, our risen Lord.
~Amen.

READING *Matthew 28:1–6*

After the Sabbath, as the first day of the week
was dawning, Mary Magdalene and the other
Mary went to see the tomb. And suddenly there
was a great earthquake; for an angel of the
Lord, descending from heaven, came and rolled
back the stone and sat on it. His appearance was

like lightning, and his clothing white as snow.
For fear of him the guards shook and became
like dead men. But the angel said to the women,
"Do not be afraid; I know that you are looking
for Jesus who was crucified. He is not here;
for he has been raised, as he said. Come, see the
place where he lay."

SILENCE

RESPONSE

The stone that the builders rejected, alleluia!
~Has become the cornerstone, alleluia!

CANTICLE OF ZACHARY *Luke 1:67–7*

*You are looking for Jesus of Nazareth, who was
crucified. He has been raised; he is not here,
alleluia!*

Blessed are you, + Lord, the God of Israel,
you have come to your people and set them free.
You have raised up for us a mighty Savior,
born of the house of your servant David.

Through your holy prophets, you promised
    of old
to save us from our enemies,
from the hands of all who hate us,
to show mercy to our forebears,
and to remember your holy covenant.

This was the oath you swore
  to our father Abraham:
to set us free from the hands of our enemies,
free to worship you without fear,
holy and righteous before you,
all the days of our life.

And you, child, shall be called the prophet
  of the Most High,
for you will go before the Lord to prepare
  the way,
to give God's people knowledge of salvation
by the forgiveness of their sins.

In the tender compassion of our God
the dawn from on high shall break upon us,
to shine on those who dwell in darkness
  and the shadow of death,
and to guide our feet into the way of peace.

Glory to the holy and undivided Trinity:
now and always and for ever and ever. Amen.

LORD'S PRAYER

CLOSING PRAYER

Lord Jesus Christ,
you snapped the bonds of death
and rose a victor from the grave.
Put away our sins,

restore innocence to the guilty
and joy to the disheartened,
and bring us out of the prison-house of death
into your paradise for ever green,
where you live and reign for ever and ever.
~*Amen.*

May the risen Christ, our gracious Savior,
+ bless us and keep us.
~*Amen.*

MONDAY EVENING

Jesus Christ + is the light of the world.
~*A light no darkness can extinguish.*

Christ is risen, alleluia!
~*He is risen indeed, alleluia!*

HYMN

PSALM 114

*All of us who have been baptized into Christ
Jesus have been baptized into his death, alleluia!*

When Israel came forth from Egypt,
Jacob's family from an alien people,
Judah became the Lord's temple,
Israel became God's kingdom.

The sea fled at the sight,
the Jordan turned back on its course,
the mountains leapt like rams
and the hills like yearling sheep.

Why was it, sea, that you fled,
that you turned back, Jordan, in your course?
Mountains, that you leapt like rams;
hills, like yearling sheep?

Tremble, O earth, before the LORD,
in the presence of the God of Jacob,
who turns the rock into a pool
and flint into a spring of water.

PSALM PRAYER

Rescuing God,
of old you brought forth your chosen people
from the slavery of Egypt
and conducted them across the Jordan
into a land flowing with milk and honey.
Deliver now the people of the new covenant
from the slavery of sin
and make your church a land of spiritual plenty,
through Jesus Christ, our risen Lord.
~*Amen.*

READING   *1 Peter 1:3–5*

Blessed be the God and Father of our Lord Jesus
Christ! By his great mercy he has given us a

new birth into a living hope through the resurrection of Jesus Christ from the dead, and into an inheritance that is imperishable, undefiled, and unfading, kept in heaven for you, who are being protected by the power of God through faith for a salvation ready to be revealed in the last time.

SILENCE

RESPONSE

Christ died for our sins and was buried, alleluia!
~*And was raised to life on the third day, alleluia!*

CANTICLE OF MARY *Luke 1:46–55*

Jesus said to Thomas, "Blessed are those who have not seen and yet have come to believe," alleluia!

My soul **+** proclaims the greatness of the Lord,
my spirit rejoices in God my Savior,
for you, Lord, have looked with favor on your
    lowly servant.

From this day all generations will call me
    blessed:
you, the Almighty, have done great things for me
and holy is your name.

You have mercy on those who fear you,
from generation to generation.

You have shown strength with your arm
and scattered the proud in their conceit,
casting down the mighty from their thrones
and lifting up the lowly.
You have filled the hungry with good things
and sent the rich away empty.

You have come to the aid of your servant Israel,
to remember the promise of mercy,
the promise made to our forebears,
to Abraham and his children for ever.

Glory to God: Creator, Redeemer, and Sanctifier,
now and always and for ever and ever. Amen.

INTERCESSIONS

Lord Jesus, our life and our resurrection:
~*Lord, have mercy.*

Lord Jesus, who established the new and eternal
covenant in your precious blood:
~*Lord, have mercy.*

Lord Jesus, who set us free from the law of sin
and death:
~*Lord, have mercy.*

Lord Jesus, pleading for us at God's right hand:
~*Lord, have mercy.*

Lord Jesus, hope of the faithful departed:
~*Lord, have mercy.*

By the prayers of the great Mother of God,
Mary most holy, and of all the saints:
~*Lord, have mercy.*

LORD'S PRAYER

CLOSING PRAYER

Heavenly Father,
for us and for our salvation
you delivered up your only Son
to the death of the cross,
and by his glorious resurrection
rescued us from the power of the enemy.
Help us to die daily to sin
that we may always walk in newness of life
in the power and glory of his risen existence,
through the same Christ our Lord.
~*Amen.*

May the blessing of almighty God,
the Father, the Son, and the Holy Spirit,
+ descend upon us and remain with us for ever.
~*Amen.*

AN EVENING ANTHEM TO MARY DURING EASTER, *page 229*

O Lord, **+** open my lips.
~*And my mouth shall declare your praise.*

There are shouts of joy and victory, alleluia!
~*In the tents of the just, alleluia!*

HYMN

PSALM 118:1, 5–9, 13–17, 22–25

This day was made by the Lord; we rejoice and are glad, alleluia!

Give thanks to the LORD who is good,
for God's love endures for ever.
Let those who fear the LORD say:
"God's love endures for ever."

I called to the LORD in my distress;
God answered and freed me.
The LORD is at my side; I do not fear.
What can mortals do against me?
The LORD is at my side as my helper;
I shall look down on my foes.

It is better to take refuge in the LORD
than to trust in mortals;
it is better to take refuge in the LORD
than to trust in rulers.

I was thrust down, thrust down and falling,
but the LORD was my helper.
The LORD is my strength and my song;
and has been my savior.
There are shouts of joy and victory
in the tents of the just.

The LORD's right hand has triumphed;
God's right hand raised me.
The LORD's right hand has triumphed;
I shall not die, I shall live
and recount God's deeds.

The stone which the builders rejected
has become the corner stone.
This is the work of the LORD,
a marvel in our eyes.
This day was made by the LORD;
we rejoice and are glad.

O LORD, grant us salvation;
O LORD, grant success.

PSALM PRAYER

Abba, dear Father,
by the risen Christ whom we praise,
who slept that we might keep watch
and who died that we might live,
grant us the grace to reign with him

in the life that knows no end,
through the same Christ our Lord.
~*Amen.*

READING   *Matthew 28:8–10*

The three women left the tomb quickly with
fear and great joy, and ran to tell his disciples.
Suddenly Jesus met them and said, "Greetings!"
And they came to him, took hold of his feet,
and worshipped him. Then Jesus said to them,
"Do not be afraid; go and tell my brothers to go
to Galilee; there they will see me."

SILENCE

RESPONSE

The Lord is risen indeed, alleluia!
~*And has appeared to Simon Peter, alleluia!*

CANTICLE OF JEREMIAH
Jeremiah 31:10–13

*This Jesus God raised up and made him both
Lord and Messiah, alleluia!*

Hear the word of the LORD, O nations,
and declare it in the coastlands far away;
say, "He who scattered Israel will gather him,
and will keep him as a shepherd a flock."

For the LORD has ransomed Jacob,
and has redeemed him from hands too strong
for him.
They shall come and sing aloud on the height
of Zion,
and they shall be radiant over the goodness
of the LORD,

over the grain, the wine, and the oil,
and over the young of the flock and the herd;
their life shall become like a watered garden,
and they shall never languish again.

Then shall the young women rejoice
in the dance,
and the young men and the old shall be merry.
I will turn their mourning into joy,
I will comfort them, and give them gladness
for sorrow.

To the Ruler of the ages, immortal, invisible,
the only wise God,
be honor and glory, through Jesus Christ,
for ever and ever. Amen.

LORD'S PRAYER

CLOSING PRAYER

Lord Jesus Christ,
by your cross and resurrection,

you destroyed death
and brought life to those in the grave.
May your blessed passion be the joy of the
   whole world
and may the glory of your rising from the tomb
ever be our song,
O Savior of the world,
living and reigning with the Father
   and the Holy Spirit,
now and for ever.
~*Amen.*

May the risen Lord **+** be with us
now and for ever.
~*Amen.*

TUESDAY EVENING

Light and peace **+** in Jesus Christ our Lord.
~*Thanks be to God.*

Christ is risen, alleluia!
~*He is risen indeed, alleluia!*

HYMN

PSALM 76

Christ was raised from the dead by the glory of the Father, alleluia!

God, you are known in Judah;
in Israel your name is great.
You set up your tent in Jerusalem
and your dwelling place in Zion.
It was there you broke the flashing arrows,
the shield, the sword, the armor.

You, O Lord, are resplendent,
more majestic than the everlasting mountains.
The warriors, despoiled, slept in death;
the hands of the soldiers were powerless.
At your threat, O God of Jacob,
horse and rider lay stunned.

You, you alone, strike terror.
Who shall stand when your anger is roused?
You uttered your sentence from the heavens;
the earth in terror was still
when you arose to judge,
to save the humble of the earth.

Human anger will serve to praise you;
those who survive it rejoice in you.
Make vows to your God and fulfill them.
Let all pay tribute to the one who strikes terror,
who cuts short the breath of rulers,
who strikes terror in the leaders of the earth.

Psalm Prayer

Lord Jesus Christ,
when the Father raised you from the dead
to save the humble of the earth,
the guards trembled and became like dead men.
Make us who believe and trust in your
    resurrection
confident of our victory over death and the grave
by the glorious power of your Father.
You live and reign now and for ever.
~*Amen.*

READING   *1 Peter 1:18–21*

Sisters and brothers, you know that you were
ransomed from the futile ways inherited
from your ancestors, not with perishable things
like silver or gold, but with the precious blood
of Christ, like that of a lamb without defect
or blemish. He was destined before the founda-
tion of the world, but was revealed at the end
of the ages for your sake. Through him you have
come to trust in God, who raised him from
the dead and gave him glory, so that your faith
and hope are set on God.

SILENCE

RESPONSE

God has given us a new birth into a living hope,
alleluia!
~*Through the resurrection of Jesus Christ from
the dead, alleluia!*

CANTICLE OF THE VICTORIOUS CROSS

*Holy God, holy mighty One, holy immortal
One, have mercy on us.*

We adore you, Lord Jesus Christ, as you ascend
your cross.
May this cross deliver us from the destroying
angel.

We adore your pierced and wounded body as it
hangs on the cross.
May your wounds be our healing.

We adore you dead and buried in the tomb.
May your death be our life.

We adore you as you descend among the dead
to deliver them.
May we never hear the dread sentence of doom.

We adore you rising gloriously from the dead.
Free us from the weight of our sins.

We adore you ascending to the right hand
of the Father.
Raise us to eternal glory with all your saints.

We adore you coming to judge the living and
the dead.
At your coming be not our judge but our Savior.

INTERCESSIONS

Lord Jesus, victor over death and hell, crush
beneath your feet the prince of darkness and all
his powers:
~*Hear us, risen Lord.*

Lord Jesus, grant us victory over all our
enemies, seen and unseen:
~*Hear us, risen Lord.*

Lord Jesus, raise us from the tomb of our sins
and offenses:
~*Hear us, risen Lord.*

Lord Jesus, fill us with the joy and happiness of
your resurrection:
~*Hear us, risen Lord.*

Lord Jesus, conduct us to your wedding banquet
to rejoice with all your saints:
~*Hear us, risen Lord.*

By the prayers of the great Mother of God,
Mary most holy, and of all the saints:
~Hear us, risen Lord.

LORD'S PRAYER

CLOSING PRAYER

Holy and splendid cross,
you are more exalted than all the trees
   of the forest.
On you hung the life of the world,
on you Christ proceeded to his triumph,
on you death overcame death.
By the precious blood that anointed the cross,
may we be delivered from all sin and danger
and made true disciples of Jesus crucified,
today and every day and through all
   the ages of ages.
~Amen.

By the precious and life-giving cross,
may our risen Lord + save and deliver us.
~Amen.

AN EVENING ANTHEM TO MARY DURING EASTER, *page 229*

O Lord, **+** open my lips.
~And my mouth shall declare your praise.

Christ trampled down death by his death,
alleluia!
~And brought life to those in the grave, alleluia!

HYMN

PSALM 66:1–9, 12, 16–17, 20

Lord Jesus, how tremendous are your deeds!

Cry out with joy to God all the earth,
O sing to the glory of his name
rendering glorious praise.
Say to God: "How tremendous your deeds!

Because of the greatness of your strength
your enemies cringe before you.
Before you all the earth shall bow,
shall sing to you, sing to your name!"

Come and see the works of God,
tremendous deeds for the people.
God turned the sea into dry land,
they passed through the river dry-shod.

Let our joy then be in the Lord,
who rules forever in power,
whose eyes keep watch over nations;
let rebels not lift themselves up.

O people, bless our God;
let the voice of God's praise resound,
of the God who gave life to our souls
and kept our feet from stumbling.

You let foes ride over our heads;
we went through fire and through water
but then you brought us relief.

Come and hear, all who fear God,
I will tell what God did for my soul;
to God I cried aloud,
with high praise ready on my tongue.

Blessed be God who has not rejected my prayer
nor withheld his love from me.

Psalm Prayer

God of glory,
by the preaching of the gospel
make your wonderful acts known
   to the whole world
so that all nations may praise your name,
now and for ever.
~*Amen.*

READING   *Matthew 28:16–20*

Now the eleven disciples went to Galilee, to
the mountain to which Jesus had directed them.
When they saw him, they worshipped him;
but some doubted. And Jesus came and said to
them, "All authority in heaven and on earth
has been given to me. Go therefore and make
disciples of all nations, baptizing them in
the name of the Father and of the Son and of
the Holy Spirit, and teaching them to obey
everything that I have commanded you. And
remember, I am with you always, to the end of
the age."

SILENCE

RESPONSE

Thanks be to God who gives us the victory,
alleluia!
~*Through our Lord Jesus Christ, alleluia!*

CANTICLE OF THE CHURCH

We praise you, O God,
we acclaim you as Lord;
all creation worships you,
the Father everlasting.

To you all angels, all the powers of heaven,
the cherubim and seraphim, sing
    in endless praise:
Holy, holy, holy Lord, God of power and might,
heaven and earth are full of your glory.

The glorious company of apostles praise you.
The noble fellowship of prophets praise you.
The white-robed army of martyrs praise you.

Throughout the world the holy Church
    acclaims you:
Father, of majesty unbounded,
your true and only Son, worthy of all praise,
and the Holy Spirit, advocate and guide.

You, Christ, are the king of glory,
the eternal Son of the Father.
When you took our flesh to set us free
you humbly chose the Virgin's womb.

You overcame the sting of death
and opened the kingdom of heaven
    to all believers.
You are seated at God's right hand in glory.
We believe that you will come to be our judge.

Come then, Lord, and help your people,
bought with the price of your own blood,
and bring us with your saints
to glory everlasting.

LORD'S PRAYER

CLOSING PRAYER

Creator and Savior of humanity,
worthy of all praise and thanksgiving,
you have established your church
on the rock of faith in your risen Son.
Increase our faith and hope
and unite us in the bonds of love and peace,
through the same Christ our Lord.
~*Amen.*

Peace **+** be to all who are in Christ.
~*Amen.*

WEDNESDAY EVENING

Light and peace **+** in Jesus Christ our Lord.
~*Thanks be to God.*

I know that my Redeemer lives, alleluia!
~*And in my flesh I shall see God, alleluia!*

HYMN

PSALM 68:2-7, 19-21

The just shall exult and dance for joy, alleluia!

Let God arise, let the foes be scattered.
Let those who hate God take flight.
As smoke is blown away so will they be
   blown away;
like wax that melts before the fire,
so the wicked shall perish at the presence
   of God.

But the just shall rejoice at the presence of God,
they shall exult and dance for joy.
O sing to the Lord, make music to God's name;
make a highway for the One who rides
   on the clouds.
rejoice in the LORD, exult before God.

Father of the orphan, defender of the widow,
such is God in the holy place.
God gives the lonely a home to live in;
and leads the prisoners forth into freedom;
but rebels must dwell in a parched land.

You have gone up on high; you have
   taken captives,
receiving people in tribute, O God,
even those who rebel, into your dwelling,
   O LORD.

May the Lord be blessed day after day.
God our savior bears our burdens;
this God of ours is a God who saves.
The LORD our God holds the keys of death.

PSALM PRAYER

Merciful and loving Father,
you rescued your only Son from the grave
and made him a source of salvation for all
    who believe.
Forgive our sins, heal our diseases,
deliver the oppressed
and be the key that opens the gates of death
for all those who die in Christ.
In Jesus' name.
~*Amen.*

READING   *1 Peter 2:4–6*

Brothers and sisters, Come to Christ, a living
stone, though rejected by mortals yet chosen and
precious in God's sight, and like living stones,
let yourselves be built into a spiritual house, to
be a holy priesthood, to offer spiritual sacrifices
acceptable to God through Jesus Christ. For
it stands in scripture: "See, I am laying in Zion
a stone, a cornerstone chosen and precious;
and whoever believes in him will not be put
to shame."

SILENCE

RESPONSE

If we die with Christ, alleluia!
~*We shall also live with Christ, alleluia!*

CANTICLE FOR EASTER
1 Corinthians 5:7–8; Romans 6:9–11;
1 Corinthians 15:20–21

Alleluia, alleluia, alleluia!

Christ our Passover has been sacrificed for us;
Therefore let us keep the feast,
Not with the old leaven, the leaven of malice
   and evil,
but with the unleavened bread of sincerity
   and truth. Alleluia.

Christ being raised from the dead will
   never die again;
death no longer has dominion over him.
The death he died, he died to sin, once for all;
but the life he lives, he lives to God.
So also consider yourselves dead to sin,
and alive to God in Jesus Christ our Lord.
   Alleluia.

Christ has been raised from the dead,
the first fruits of those who have fallen asleep.
For since by a man came death,

by a man has come also the resurrection of
　the dead.
For as in Adam all die,
so also in Christ shall all be made alive. Alleluia.

Glory to the Father, and to the Son,
and to the Holy Spirit:
as it was in the beginning, is now,
and will be for ever. Amen.

INTERCESSIONS

Lord Jesus, light and salvation of all peoples:
~*Show us your mercy and love.*

Lord Jesus, always standing and interceding
for us:
~*Show us your mercy and love.*

Lord Jesus, the same yesterday, today, and
for ever:
~*Show us your mercy and love.*

Lord Jesus, consolation of the persecuted
and afflicted:
~*Show us your mercy and love.*

Lord Jesus, light and peace for our beloved dead:
~*Show us your mercy and love.*

By the prayers of the great mother of God,
Mary most holy, and of all the saints:
~*Show us your mercy and love.*

LORD'S PRAYER

CLOSING PRAYER

Good Shepherd of the flock,
you rescued your dear Son from the valley
    of death
and anointed him as Messiah and Lord.
May we drink from the overflowing cup
    of the Spirit
and dwell in your house all the days of our life,
for the sake of Jesus our Savior.
~*Amen.*

May the grace of our Lord Jesus Christ
+ be with us all.
~*Amen.*

AN EVENING ANTHEM TO MARY DURING EASTER, *page 229*

THURSDAY MORNING

O Lord, + open my lips.
~*And my mouth shall declare your praise.*

The stone which the builders rejected, alleluia!
~*Has become the cornerstone, alleluia!*

HYMN

PSALM 47

Christ ascended far above all the heavens so that he might fill all things, alleluia!

All peoples clap your hands,
cry to God with shouts of joy!
For the LORD, the Most High, we must fear,
great king over all the earth.

God subdues peoples under us
and nations under our feet.
Our inheritance, our glory, is from God,
given to Jacob out of love.

God goes up with shouts of joy;
the Lord goes up with trumpet blast.
Sing praise for God, sing praise,
sing praise to our king, sing praise.

God is king of all the earth,
sing praise with all your skill.
God is king over the nations;
God reigns enthroned in holiness.

The leaders of the people are assembled
with the people of Abraham's God.
The rulers of the earth belong to God,
to God who reigns over all.

PSALM PRAYER

Almighty and everlasting God,
grant that we who believe that your Son
ascended into heaven
and now sits at your right hand,
may ourselves dwell amid heavenly things,
through the same Christ our Lord.
~Amen.

READING   *Luke 24:44, 46–49a*

Jesus said to his disciples: "Everything written
about me in the law of Moses, the prophets, and
the psalms must be fulfilled that the Messiah
is to suffer and to rise from the dead on the third
day, and that repentance and the forgiveness
of sins is to be proclaimed in his name to all
nations, beginning from Jerusalem. You are
witnesses of these things. And see, I am sending
upon you what my Father promised."

SILENCE

RESPONSE

God goes up with shouts of joy, alleluia!
~The Lord goes up with trumpet blast, alleluia!

CANTICLE OF ISAIAH   *Isaiah 12:2–6*

*The Messiah had to suffer and be raised from
the dead on the third day, alleluia!*

Behold God is my salvation;
I will trust and will not be afraid,
for the Lord God is my strength and my song;
and has become my salvation.

With joy you will draw water from the wells
    of salvation:
and in that day you will say,
"Give thanks and call upon the name
    of the Lord;
make known among the nations what the Lord
    has done, proclaim that the name of the
    LORD is exalted.

"Sing praises for the Lord has done gloriously:
let this be known in all the earth.
Shout and sing for joy you people of God:
for great in your midst is the Holy One."

Glory to you, Source of all being,
Eternal Word, and Holy Spirit:
as it was in the beginning, is now,
and will be for ever. Amen.

LORD'S PRAYER

CLOSING PRAYER

O King of glory and Lord of hosts,
who ascended in triumph above the heavens,
do not leave us orphans,
but send us the Promised of the Father,
the Spirit of truth.
Blessed be the holy and undivided Trinity,
now and for ever.
~Amen.

May the grace and blessing of the risen Lord
+ be with us all.
~Amen.

THURSDAY EVENING

Jesus Christ + is the light of the world.
~A light no darkness can extinguish.

Christ is risen, alleluia!
~He is risen indeed, alleluia!

HYMN

PSALM 111

Christ has been raised from the dead, the first
fruits of those who have died, alleluia!

I will thank the LORD with all my heart
in the meeting of the just and their assembly.
Great are the works of the LORD,
to be pondered by all who love them.

Majestic and glorious God's work,
whose justice stands firm for ever.
God makes us remember these wonders.
The LORD is compassion and love.

God gives food to those who fear him;
keeps his covenant ever in mind;
shows mighty works to his people
by giving them the land of the nations.

God's works are justice and truth,
God's precepts are all of them sure,
standing firm for ever and ever;
they are made in uprightness and truth.

God has sent deliverance to his people
and established his covenant for ever.
Holy is God's name, to be feared.

To fear the LORD is the first stage of wisdom;
all who do so prove themselves wise.
God's praise shall last for ever!

Psalm Prayer

Abba, dear Father,
majestic and glorious is the work
you accomplished in Jesus your Son.
May we always remember your loving-kindness
and establish your covenant in our hearts
as we worship in the assemblies of your people.
In Jesus' name we ask it.
~*Amen.*

Reading   *1 Peter 2:9–10*

Sisters and brothers, You are a chosen race,
a royal priesthood, a holy nation, God's own
people, in order that you may proclaim the
mighty acts of him who called you out of darkness into his marvelous light. Once you were
not a people, but now you are God's people;
once you had not received mercy, but now you
have received mercy.

Silence

Response

Think of yourselves as dead to sin, alleluia!
~*But alive to God in Christ Jesus, alleluia!*

CANTICLE OF THE FIRSTBORN OF ALL CREATION   *Colossians 1:15–20*

Jesus withdrew from them and was carried up into heaven, alleluia!

Christ is the image of the invisible God,
the firstborn of all creation;
for in him all things in heaven and on earth
    were created,
things visible and invisible,
whether thrones or dominions, or rulers
    or powers—
all things have been created through him
    and for him.

He himself is before all things,
and in him all things hold together.
He is the head of the body, the church;
he is the beginning, the firstborn from the dead,
so that he might come to have the first place
    in everything.

For in him all the fullness of God was pleased
    to dwell
and through him God was pleased
to reconcile to himself all things,
whether on earth or in heaven,
by making peace through the blood of his cross.

Glory to the holy and undivided Trinity:
now and always and for ever and ever. Amen.

INTERCESSIONS

Lord Jesus, King of glory, sitting at the right
hand of the Father:
~*Grant us peace.*

Lord Jesus, filling the whole universe with
your presence:
~*Grant us peace.*

Lord Jesus, drawing all things to yourself:
~*Grant us peace.*

Lord Jesus, who will come again in glory
to judge the living and the dead:
~*Grant us peace.*

Lord Jesus, who promised the Spirit of truth:
~*Grant us peace.*

By the prayers of the great Mother of God,
Mary most holy, and of all the saints:
~*Grant us peace.*

LORD'S PRAYER

CLOSING PRAYER

God, our salvation,
you heard your Son when he cried out to you
and raised him out of the sleep of death.
Be with your church in its hour of need,

strengthen it with the Spirit of truth,
and lead it into the way of holiness.
We ask this in Jesus' name.
~*Amen.*

The grace of our Lord Jesus Christ, and the love
of God, and the communion of the Holy Spirit,
+ be with us all.
~*Amen.*

AN EVENING ANTHEM TO MARY DURING EASTER, *page 229*

FRIDAY MORNING

O Lord, + open my lips.
~*And my mouth shall declare your praise.*

I called to the LORD in my distress, alleluia!
~*God answered and freed me, alleluia!*

HYMN

PSALM 135:1-6, 13-20

The Lord took pity on his servant Jesus, alleluia!

Praise the name of the LORD,
praise, you servants of the LORD,
who stand in the house of the LORD
in the courts of the house of our God.

Praise the LORD for the LORD is good.
Praise God's name; God is gracious.
For Jacob has been chosen by the LORD;
Israel for God's own possession.

For I know the LORD is great,
that our Lord is high above all gods.
Whatever the LORD wills, the LORD does,
in heaven, on earth, in the seas.

LORD, your name stands for ever,
unforgotten from age to age,
for the LORD does justice for his people;
the Lord takes pity on his servants.

The pagans' idols are silver and gold,
the work of human hands.
They have mouths but they cannot speak;
they have eyes but they cannot see.

They have ears but they cannot hear;
there is never breath on their lips.
Their makers will come to be like them
and so will all who trust in them!

House of Israel, bless the LORD!
House of Aaron, bless the LORD!
House of Levi, bless the LORD!
You who fear the LORD, bless the Lord!

PSALM PRAYER

Gracious God,
you sent Jesus to proclaim the Good News
of freedom to the whole world.
Set us free from the idolatry of money
and liberate us from the desire
    to dominate others,
for the sake of Jesus our Savior.
~*Amen.*

READING   *John 20:19–23*

It was late that Sunday evening, and the disciples
were gathered together behind locked doors,
because they were afraid of the Jewish authorities. Then Jesus came and stood among them.
"Peace be with you," he said. After saying
this, he showed them his hands and his side. The
disciples were filled with joy at seeing the Lord.
Jesus said to them again, "Peace be with you.

As the Father sent me, so I send you." Then he breathed on them and said, "Receive the Holy Spirit. If you forgive people's sins, they are forgiven; if you do not forgive them, they are not forgiven."

SILENCE

RESPONSE
God raised Christ from the dead, alleluia!
~*And set him free from the pains of death, alleluia!*

CANTICLE OF ISAIAH   *Isaiah 63:1–5*

Blessed are those who have not seen and yet have come to believe, alleluia!

"Who is this who comes from Edom,
from Bozrah in garments stained crimson?
Who is this so splendidly robed,
marching in his great might?"

"It is I, announcing vindication,
mighty to save."

"Why are your robes red,
and your garments like theirs
who tread the wine press?"

"I have trodden the wine press alone,
and from the peoples no one was with me;
I trod them in my anger
and trampled them in my wrath;
their juice spattered on my garments,
and stained all my robes.

I looked, but there was no helper;
I stared, but there was no one to sustain me,
so my own arm brought me victory,
and my wrath sustained me.

Glory to God: Creator, Redeemer, and Sanctifier:
now and always and for ever and ever. Amen.

LORD'S PRAYER

CLOSING PRAYER

God of peace,
you brought our Lord Jesus back from the dead
to become the great Shepherd of the sheep
by the blood that sealed an eternal covenant.
Turn us into what is acceptable to you,
through the same Christ Jesus,
to whom be glory for ever and ever.
~*Amen.*

May grace be **+** with all who have an undying
love for our Lord Jesus Christ.
~*Amen.*

FRIDAY EVENING

Light and peace + in Jesus Christ our Lord.
~*Thanks be to God.*

Christ has risen from the dead, alleluia!
~*The first fruits of those who have fallen asleep, alleluia!*

HYMN

PSALM 86:1–10, 12–13

How great is the glory of the risen Lord!

Turn your ear, O LORD, and give answer
for I am poor and needy.
Preserve my life for I am faithful;
save the servant who trusts in you.

You are my God, have mercy on me, Lord;
for I cry to you all the day long.
Give joy to your servant, O Lord,
for to you I lift up my soul.

O Lord, you are good and forgiving,
full of love to all who call.
Give heed, O LORD, to my prayer
and attend to the sound of my voice.

In the day of distress I will call
and surely you will reply.
Among the gods there is none like you, O Lord,
nor work to compare with yours.

All the nations shall come to adore you
and glorify your name, O Lord,
for you are great and do marvelous deeds,
you who alone are God.

I will praise you, Lord, my God,
    with all my heart
and glorify your name for ever;
for your love to me has been great,
you have saved me from the depths of the grave.

Psalm Prayer

Abba, dear Father,
your love is eternal, your fidelity unceasing.
By the love you showed your only Son,
when you saved him from the grave,
stretch out your hand to save the church
that struggles to do your holy will,
through the same Christ our Lord.
~*Amen.*

READING   *1 Peter 3:18–22*

Christ suffered for sins once for all, the righteous
for the unrighteous, in order to bring you to
God. He was put to death in the flesh, but made
alive in the spirit, in which he also went and
made a proclamation to the spirits in prison,
who in former times did not obey, when God
waited patiently in the days of Noah, during
the building of the ark, in which a few, that is,
eight persons, were saved through water. And
baptism, which this prefigured, now saves
you—not as a removal of dirt from the body,
but as an appeal to God for a good conscience,
through the resurrection of Jesus Christ,
who has gone into heaven and is at the right
hand of God, with angels, authorities, and
powers made subject to him.

SILENCE

RESPONSE

God has given us new birth into a living hope:
~*Through the resurrection of Jesus Christ from
the dead.*

CANTICLE FOR EASTER
1 Corinthians 5:7–8; Romans 6:9–11;
1 Corinthians 15:20–23

Alleluia, alleluia, alleluia!

Christ our Passover has been sacrificed for us;

Therefore let us keep the feast,
Not with the old leaven, the leaven of malice
and evil,
but with the unleavened bread of sincerity
and truth. Alleluia.

Christ being raised from the dead will
never die again;
death no longer has dominion over him.
The death he died, he died to sin, once for all;
but the life he lives, he lives to God.
So also consider yourselves dead to sin,
and alive to God in Jesus Christ our Lord.
Alleluia.

Christ has been raised from the dead,
the first fruits of those who have fallen asleep.
For since by a man came death,
by a man has come also the resurrection
of the dead.
For as in Adam all die,
so also in Christ shall all be made alive. Alleluia.

Glory to the Father, and to the Son,
and to the Holy Spirit:
as it was in the beginning, is now,
and will be for ever. Amen.

INTERCESSIONS

Lord Jesus, victor over death and hell, crush
beneath your feet the prince of darkness and all
his powers:
~*Hear us, risen Lord.*

Lord Jesus, grant us victory over all our enemies,
seen and unseen:
~*Hear us, risen Lord.*

Lord Jesus, raise us from the tomb of our sins
and offenses:
·*Hear us, risen Lord.*

Lord Jesus, fill us with the joy and happiness of
your resurrection:
~*Hear us, risen Lord.*

Lord Jesus, conduct us to your wedding
banquet to rejoice with all your saints.
~*Hear us, risen Lord.*

By the prayers of the great Mother of God,
Mary most holy, and of all the saints:
~*Hear us, risen Christ.*

LORD'S PRAYER

CLOSING PRAYER

Risen and victorious Lord,
whose power is beyond compare
and whose love for us is beyond all words
   to describe,
hear the prayers of your ransomed people
and grant us the riches of your promised mercy;
for you are our light and our resurrection,
O Savior of the world,
and we glorify you, and your eternal Father,
and your holy and life-giving Spirit,
now and always and for ever and ever.
~Amen.

May God fully + satisfy every need of ours
according to his riches in Christ Jesus.
~Amen.

AN EVENING ANTHEM TO MARY DURING EASTER, *page 229*

SATURDAY MORNING

O Lord, + hear my prayer.
~And my mouth shall declare your praise.

This day was made by the Lord, alleluia!
~We rejoice and are glad, alleluia!!

HYMN

PSALM 22:23–32

*All the mighty of the earth shall bow down in
awe to the risen Christ, alleluia!*

I will tell of your name to my people
and praise you where they are assembled.
"You who fear the LORD give praise;
all children of Jacob, give glory.
Revere God, children of Israel.

For God has never despised
nor scorned the poverty of the poor,
nor looked away from them,
but has heard the poor when they cried."

You are my praise in the great assembly.
My vows I will pay before those who fear God.
The poor shall eat and have their fill.
Those who seek the LORD shall praise the LORD.
May their hearts live for ever and ever!

All the earth shall remember and return
    to the LORD,
all families of the nations shall bow down in awe;
for the kingdom is the LORD's, who is
    ruler of all.
They shall bow down in awe, all the mighty
    of the earth,
all who must die and go down to the dust.

My soul shall live for God and my children too
    shall serve.
They shall tell of the Lord to generations
    yet to come;
declare to those unborn, the faithfulness of God.
"These things the Lord has done."

PSALM PRAYER

Abba, dear Father of Jesus,
you have brought us to new birth
by water and the Holy Spirit
and have forgiven all our sins.
Anoint us with your Holy Spirit,
perfect us with the seven-fold gifts
and establish us in justice and peace,
through the same Christ our Lord.
~*Amen.*

READING   *1 Corinthians 15:1–8*

Now I would remind you, brothers and sisters,
of the good news that I proclaimed to you,
which you in turn received, through which also
you are being saved. For I handed on to you
as of the first importance what I in turn had
received: that Christ died for our sins in accordance with the scriptures, and that he was
buried, and that he was raised on the third day
in accordance with the scriptures, and that he
appeared to Cephas, then to the twelve. Then

he appeared to more than five hundred brothers
and sisters at one time, most of who are still
alive, though some have died. Then he appeared
to James, then to all the apostles. Last of all, as
to one untimely born, he appeared to me.

SILENCE

RESPONSE

The Lord Jesus was taken up to heaven, alleluia!
~*And stands at the right hand of God, alleluia!*

CANTICLE OF EZEKIEL   *Ezekiel 36:24–28*

*You shall be my people, alleluia! And I will be
your God, alleluia!*

I will take you from every nation and country
and bring you back to your own land.
I will sprinkle clean water on you
and make you clean from all your idols
and everything else that has defiled you.

I will give you a new heart and a new mind.
I will take away your stubborn heart of stone
and give you an obedient heart.

I will put my spirit in you and will see to it
that you follow my laws
and keep all the commands I have given you.

Then you will live in the land I gave your
   ancestors.
You will be my people, and I will be your God.

To the Ruler of the ages, immortal, invisible,
the only wise God,
be honor and glory, through Jesus Christ,
for ever and ever. Amen.

LORD'S PRAYER

CLOSING PRAYER

God, our heavenly Father,
in whom the minds of the faithful are united,
help us to love your commandments
and to yearn after your promises,
so that amid the changing circumstances
   of this life
we may fix our hearts where true joys are
   to be found.
We ask this through Christ our Lord.
~Amen.

May our spirit and soul and body be + kept
sound and blameless at the coming of our Lord
Jesus Christ.
~Amen.

Jesus Christ + is the light of the world.
~*A light no darkness can extinguish.*

The Lord's right hand has triumphed, alleluia!
~*God's right hand has raised me, alleluia!*

HYMN

PSALM 30:2–6, 9–13

At night there are tears but joy comes with dawn, alleluia!

I will praise you, LORD, you have rescued me
and have not let my enemies rejoice over me.

O LORD, I cried to you for help
and you, my God, have healed me.
O LORD, you have raised my soul
 from the dead,
restored me to life from those who sink
 into the grave.

Sing psalms to the LORD, you faithful ones,
give thanks to his holy name.
God's anger lasts a moment; God's favor
 all through life.
At night there are tears but joy comes
 with dawn.

To you, LORD, I cried,
to my God I made appeal:
"What profit would my death be, my going
   to the grave?
Can dust give you praise or proclaim
   your truth?"

The LORD listened and had pity.
The LORD came to my help.
For me you have changed my mourning
   into dancing,
you removed my sackcloth and clothed me
   with joy.
So my soul sings psalms to you unceasingly.
O LORD my God, I will thank you for ever.

PSALM PRAYER

Lord Jesus,
may we who celebrate the mysteries
of your passion, death and resurrection
rejoice together with all your saints
when you come again in glory
to judge the living and the dead.
You live and reign,
with the Father and the Holy Spirit,
now and for ever.
~*Amen.*

READING   *Hebrews 5:7–9*

In the days of his flesh, Jesus offered up
prayers and supplications to the one who
was ble to save him from death, and he
was heard because of his reverent submission. Although he was a Son, he learned
obedience through what he suffered;
and having been made perfect, he became
the source of eternal salvation for all
who obey him, having been designated
by God a high priest according to the
order of Melchizedek.

SILENCE

RESPONSE

Christ, our Passover lamb, has been sacrificed,
alleluia!
~*Let us celebrate the feast, alleluia!*

CANTICLE OF PAUL *Philippians 2:6–11*

Christ is the beginning, the firstborn from the dead, alleluia!

Though he was in the form of God,
Jesus did not regard equality with God
as something to be exploited,
but emptied himself,
taking the form of a slave,
being born in human likeness.

And being found in human form,
he humbled himself
and became obedient to the point of death—
even death on a cross.

Therefore God also highly exalted him
and gave him the name
that is above every name,

so that at the name of Jesus
every knee should bend,
in heaven and on earth and under the earth,
and every tongue should confess
that Jesus Christ is Lord,
to the glory of God the Father.

To the One seated on the throne and
to the Lamb
be blessing and honor and glory and might
for ever and ever. Amen.

APOSTLES' CREED

INTERCESSIONS

Lord Jesus, made obedient to the point of death,
teach us obedience:
~*Lord, have mercy.*

Lord Jesus, high priest of the new and eternal
covenant, keep us faithful in your mysteries:
~*Lord, have mercy.*

Lord Jesus, the beginning and end of God's plan,
make us servants of that design:
~*Lord, have mercy.*

Lord Jesus, purity and strength of your church,
lead your people in your ways:
~*Lord, have mercy.*

Lord Jesus, the life and hope of those who die
in you, console all those who mourn the dead:
~*Lord, have mercy.*

By the prayers of your devoted Mother
and of all your saints in glory:
~*Lord, have mercy.*

LORD'S PRAYER

CLOSING PRAYER

Heavenly Father,
you raised Jesus Christ from the dead

and made him sit at your right hand.
Rescue us from our sins,
bring us to new life in Christ,
and give us a place in heaven,
in the same Christ Jesus our Lord.
~*Amen.*

May the Lord of peace himself
give **+** us peace at all times and in all ways.
~*Amen.*

AN EVENING ANTHEM TO MARY DURING EASTER, *page 229*

Use these forms of Morning Prayer and Evening Prayer throughout the seven weeks of Easter.

PENTECOST MORNING

O Lord, **+** open my lips.
~*And my mouth shall declare your praise.*

Blessed be the Holy Spirit, our advocate and guide:
~*Who enlightens and sanctifies our souls and bodies.*

HYMN

PSALM 33:1-3, 12-22

Everyone who calls on the name of the Lord shall be saved, alleluia!

Ring out your joy to the LORD, O you just;
for praise is fitting for loyal hearts.

Give thanks to the LORD upon the harp,
with a ten-stringed lute play your songs.
Sing to the Lord a song that is new,
play loudly, with all your skill.

They are happy, whose God is the LORD,
the people who are chosen as his own.
From the heavens the LORD looks forth
and sees all the peoples of the earth.

From the heavenly dwelling God gazes
on all the dwellers on the earth;
God who shapes the hearts of them all
and considers all their deeds.

A king is not saved by his army,
nor a warrior preserved by his strength.
A vain hope for safety is the horse;
despite its power it cannot save.

The LORD looks on those who fear him,
on those who hope in his love,
to rescue their souls from death,
to keep them alive in famine.

Our soul is waiting for the LORD.
The Lord is our help and our shield.
Our hearts find joy in the Lord.
We trust in God's holy name.

May your love be upon us, O LORD,
as we place all our hope in you.

PSALM PRAYER

Divine Spirit,
guiding your people in every age,
renew now in our own days
the spirit of preaching and prophecy
that will enlighten and inspire
those who put their trust in you.
In Jesus' name.
~Amen.

READING   *Ezekiel 37:9–10*

Then the LORD said to me, "Prophesy to the
breath, prophesy, mortal, and say to the breath:
Thus says the Lord GOD: Come from the
four winds, O breath, and breathe upon these
slain, that they may live." I prophesied as

he commanded me, and the breath came into
them, and they lived, and stood on their feet,
a vast multitude.

SILENCE

RESPONSE

I shall cause the breath to enter you, alleluia!
~*And you shall live, alleluia!*

CANTICLE OF THE THREE YOUTHS
Daniel 3:52–57

Blest be the Holy Spirit, our comforter and guide!

Blest are you, Lord, God of our ancestors,
praised and glorified above all for ever!
Blest be your holy and wonderful name,
praised and glorified above all for ever!

Blest are you in your temple of glory,
praised and glorified above all for ever!
Blest are you on your heavenly throne,
praised and glorified above all for ever!

Blest are you enthroned on the cherubim,
praised and glorified above all for ever!
Blest are you who look into the depths,
praised and glorified above all for ever!

Blest are you in the heavenly vault,
praised and glorified above all for ever!
Blest be the Father, the Son, and the Holy Spirit,
praised and glorified above all for ever!

APOSTLES' CREED

LORD'S PRAYER

CLOSING PRAYER

God of fire and light,
on the first Pentecost
you instructed the hearts of believers
by the light of the Holy Spirit.
Under the inspiration of that same Spirit,
give us a taste for what is right and true
and a continuing sense
of God's presence and power in our lives,
through Jesus Christ our Lord.
~*Amen.*

May the blessing of almighty God,
the Father, the Son, and the Holy Spirit,
+ descend on us and remain with us for ever.
~*Amen.*

Jesus Christ + is the light of the world.
~A light no darkness can extinguish.

Come, Spirit of truth, alleluia!
~And guide us into all truth, alleluia!

HYMN

PSALM 104:1–2, 24–34

*You send forth your Spirit, alleluia! and renew
the face of the earth, alleluia!*

Bless the LORD, my soul!
LORD God, how great you are,
clothed in majesty and glory,
wrapped in light as in a robe!

How many are your works, O LORD!
In wisdom you have made them all.
The earth is full of your riches.

There is the sea, vast and wide,
with its moving swarms past counting,
living things great and small.
The ships are moving there
and the monsters you made to play with.

All of these look to you
to give them their food in due season.
You give it, they gather it up;
you open your hand, they have their fill.

You hide your face, they are dismayed;
you take back your spirit, they die,
returning to the dust from which they came.
You send forth your spirit, they are created;
and you renew the face of the earth.

May the glory of the LORD last for ever!
May the LORD rejoice in creation!
God looks on the earth and it trembles;
at God's touch, the mountains send forth smoke.

I will sing to the LORD all my life,
make music to my God while I live.
May my thoughts be pleasing to God.
I find my joy in the LORD.

PSALM PRAYER

Lord God of all creation,
in the beginning your Spirit brooded over
    the waters
and brought forth a world of bounty and beauty.
In these final days may the same Spirit
come to create and inspire us afresh

and renew the face of the earth.
We ask this through Christ our Lord.
~Amen.

READING   *Acts 2:1–4*

When the day of Pentecost had come, they were
all together in one place. And suddenly from
heaven there came a sound like the rush of a
violent wind and it filled the entire house where
they were sitting. Divided tongues, as of fire,
appeared among them, and a tongue rested
on each of them. All of them were filled with
the Holy Spirit and began to speak in other
languages, as the Spirit gave them ability.

Silence

Response

The Holy Spirit will teach you all things, alleluia!
~And lead you into all truth, alleluia!

CANTICLE OF MARY   *Luke 1:46–55*

*Come, Holy Spirit, fill the hearts of your faithful
and kindle in them the fire of your love, alleluia!*

My soul **+** proclaims the greatness of the Lord,
my spirit rejoices in God my Savior,
for you, Lord, have looked with favor on your
    lowly servant.

From this day all generations will call me
    blessed:
you, the Almighty, have done great things for me
and holy is your name.
You have mercy on those who fear you,
from generation to generation.

You have shown strength with your arm
and scattered the proud in their conceit,
casting down the mighty from their thrones
and lifting up the lowly.
You have filled the hungry with good things
and sent the rich away empty.

You have come to the aid of your servant Israel,
to remember the promise of mercy,
the promise made to our forebears,
to Abraham and his children for ever.

Glory to the Father, and to the Son,
and to the Holy Spirit:
as it was in the beginning, is now,
and will be for ever. Amen.

INTERCESSIONS

Lord and life-giving Spirit, you brooded over
the primeval waters:
~*Come, fill our hearts.*

You led your people Israel out of slavery
and into the freedom of the children of God:
~*Come, fill our hearts.*

You overshadowed Mary of Nazareth
and by her consent made her the Mother of God:
~*Come, fill our hearts.*

You anointed Jesus as Messiah when he was
baptized by John in the Jordan:
~*Come, fill our hearts.*

You raised Jesus out of death and proclaimed
him Son of God in all his power:
~*Come, fill our hearts.*

You appeared in tongues of flame on Pentecost
and endowed your disciples with divine gifts:
~*Come, fill our hearts.*

You send us out to testify to the Good News
about Jesus the Christ:
~*Come, fill our hearts.*

By the prayers of the great Mother of God, Mary
most holy, and of the whole company of heaven:
~*Come, fill our hearts.*

LORD'S PRAYER

CLOSING PRAYER

Heavenly King, Consoler, Spirit of truth,
present in all places and filling all things,
treasury of blessings and giver of life:
Come and dwell in us,
cleanse us from every stain of sin,
and save our souls,
O gracious Lord.
~*Amen.*

May the grace of our Lord Jesus Christ,
and the love of God, and the communion of the
Holy Spirit + be with us now and for ever.
~*Amen.*

AN EVENING ANTHEM TO MARY DURING EASTER, *page 229*

NIGHT PRAYER

Night Prayer *(Compline)* was originally recited in the dormitories of monasteries just before going to bed. It is suitable for single people, couples, families or church groups who wish to round out a full day of work and play.

This order for Night Prayer follows the format of Morning and Evening prayer. Three psalms and three readings have been provided. Choose one of each.

Our help + is in the name of the Lord.
~*The maker of heaven and earth.*

Even darkness is not dark for you, O Lord.
~*And night is clear as day.*

PSALM 31:2-6

In you, O LORD, I take refuge.
Let me never be put to shame.
In your justice, set me free,
hear me and speedily rescue me.

Be a rock of refuge for me,
a mighty stronghold to save me,
for you are my rock, my stronghold.
For your name's sake, lead me and guide me.

Release me from the snares they have hidden
for you are my refuge, Lord.
Into your hands I commend my spirit.
It is you who will redeem me, LORD.

PSALM 131

O LORD, my heart is not proud
nor haughty my eyes.
I have not gone after things too great
nor marvels beyond me.

Truly I have set my soul
in silence and peace.
A weaned child on its mother's breast,
even so is my soul.

O Israel, hope in the LORD
both now and for ever.

PSALM 133

How good and how pleasant it is,
when people live in unity!

It is like precious oil upon the head,
running down upon the beard,
running down upon Aaron's beard,
upon the collar of his robes.

It is like the dew of Hermon which falls
on the heights of Zion.
For there the LORD gives blessing,
life for ever.

DOXOLOGY

To the Ruler of the ages, immortal, invisible,
the only wise God,
be honor and glory, through Jesus Christ,
for ever and ever. Amen.

READING   *Matthew 11:28–30*

Come to me, all you that are weary and are
carrying heavy burdens, and I will give you rest.
Take my yoke upon you, and learn from me; for
I am gentle and humble in heart, and you will
find rest for your souls. For my yoke is easy,
and my burden is light.

READING   *1 Peter 5:6–9*

Humble yourselves under the mighty hand
of God, so that he may exalt you in due time.
Cast all your anxiety on him, because he cares
for you. Discipline yourselves, keep alert.
Like a roaring lion your adversary the devil
prowls around, looking for someone to devour.
Resist him, steadfast in your faith, for you know
that your brothers and sisters in all the world
are undergoing the same kind of suffering.

READING   *Jeremiah 14:9b*

You, O LORD, are in the midst of us, and we are
called by your name; do not forsake us!

RESPONSE

Into your hands, O Lord, I commend my spirit:
~*You who will redeem me, Lord, God of truth.*

CANTICLE OF SIMEON   *Luke 2:29–32*

*Jesus Christ is the light of the world, a light no
darkness can conceal.*

Now, Lord, + you let your servant go in peace:
your word has been fulfilled.

My own eyes have seen the salvation
which you have prepared in the sight of every
    people:

a light to reveal you to the nations
and the glory of your people Israel.

Glory to the Father, and to the Son,
and to the Holy Spirit:
as it was in the beginning, is now,
and will be for ever. Amen.

LORD'S PRAYER

CLOSING PRAYER

Guard us, O Lord, while we are awake
and keep us while we sleep,
that waking, we may watch with Christ,
and sleeping, we may rest in peace.
In Jesus' name.
~*Amen.*

MARIAN ANTHEMS

MARIAN ANTHEMS FOR ADVENT AND CHRISTMAS SEASON

Mother of Christ, our hope, our patroness,
star of the sea, our beacon in distress.
Guide to the shores of everlasting day
God's holy people on their pilgrim way.

Virgin, in you God made his dwelling-place;
Mother of all the living, full of grace,
blessed are you: God's word you did believe;
"Yes" on your lips undid the "No" of Eve.

Daughter of God, who bore his holy One,
dearest of all to Christ, your loving Son,
show us his face, O Mother, as on earth,
loving us all, you gave our Savior birth.

The Word was made flesh:
~*And lived among us.*

Abba, dear Father,
by the fruitful virginity of the Virgin Mary
you brought life and salvation
to all humanity.
Grant that we may experience
the power of her intercession
through whom we received the author of life,
our Lord Jesus Christ,
who lives and reigns with you
    and the Holy Spirit,
one God, for ever and ever.
~*Amen.*

May the Virgin Mary mild
 + bless us with her holy Child.
~*Amen.*

MARIAN ANTHEMS FOR LENT

We turn to you for protection,
holy Mother of God.
Listen to our prayers
and help us in our needs.
Save us from every danger,
glorious and blessed Virgin.

May we praise you, O holy Virgin.
~*Give us strength in our hour of need.*

Merciful God and Father,
may we who honor the memory
of the great Mother of God, Mary most holy,

rise from our sins by the help of her prayers.
In the name of Jesus.
~*Amen.*

May Christ, Son of God and Son of Mary,
+ bless us and keep us.
~*Amen.*

MARIAN ANTHEMS FOR EASTER SEASON

Rejoice, O Queen of heaven, alleluia!
For the Son you bore, alleluia!
Has arisen as he promised, alleluia!
Pray for us to God the Father, alleluia!

Rejoice and be glad, alleluia!
~*For the Lord has truly risen, alleluia!*

Holy and living God,
joy came into the world
when you lifted your dear Son
from among the dead.
By the prayers of Mary his mother
and of all the myrrh-bearing women,
bring us to the happiness of everlasting life,
through the same Christ our Lord.
~*Amen.*

By the power of Christ's resurrection
and the prayers of the whole company of heaven,
may God + grant us safety and peace.
~*Amen.*

APPENDIX

BIBLICAL READINGS
THROUGHOUT THE
LITURGICAL YEAR

INTRODUCTION

The following Bible readings may take the place of the shorter lessons printed in the hours for each season. No set length is suggested, but "less is more" because scripture is to be pondered, meditated and digested— not merely read. Modern Bibles usually supply divisions and headings to the text that help the reader select passages of suitable length for daily reading.

Many Bibles also have introductions to each book. These can be helpful when beginning any book that is unfamiliar. Serious students of scripture also need to consult standard introductions and commentaries on the Bible, as well as Bible dictionaries and atlases. Studying scripture in this way prepares us to hear the scripture readings more fruitfully in the liturgy. Our approach to scripture during study is different from our approach during prayer. Hearing scripture in the context of morning and evening prayer stirs up our affections so that we can reach out to the God of love who is revealed in the sacred pages. Study is useful; prayer is necessary.

ADVENT

For about four weeks before Christmas we reflect on scripture that helps us watch and pray for the coming of the Lord.

During the first three weeks choose verses from the prophet Isaiah, the Old Testament "evangelist," who supplies the most appropriate readings for this season of longing and waiting: chapters 1–14, 24–39, 40–55, 60–66.

On the eight days before Christmas, read these passages: December 17: *Isaiah 7:1–17;* December 18: *Isaiah 9:1–7;* December 19: *Isaiah 11:1–9;* December 20: *Isaiah 12:1–6;* December 21: *Isaiah 25:6–12;* December 22: *Isaiah 35:1–10;* December 23: *Isaiah 40:1–11;* December 24: *Isaiah 42:1–9.*

CHRISTMAS SEASON

Although many keep the season from December 25 to the Baptism of the Lord, the scripture readings for the Presentation of the Lord on February 2 seem to close the infancy narratives, so we might continue in the Christmas spirit until then.

Use selections from the first two chapters of the gospels of Matthew and Luke for the Christmas to Epiphany period. Read chapters 60–66 of Isaiah, and Paul's letter to the Romans for the rest of the season.

These special days should have distinctive readings: Christmas Day (December 25): *Isaiah 11:1–10;* New Year's Day (January 1): *Hebrews 2:9–17;* Epiphany:

Isaiah 60:1–6; Baptism of the Lord: *Isaiah 61:1–11* or *John 1:19–34;* Presentation of the Lord (February 2): *Malachi 3:1–7.*

LENT AND THE PASCHAL TRIDUUM

On Ash Wednesday read *Isaiah 58: 1–14* or *Joel 2:12–17.* During the season (from Ash Wednesday to Holy Thursday night) read through Exodus and Jeremiah, Mark's gospel and Paul's letter to the Hebrews.

On Palm Sunday the church reads the passion narratives from the gospels of Matthew (chapters 21–27), Mark (chapters 11–15) or Luke (chapters 22–23). These would be fruitful passages for morning and evening prayer during the next several days. On Holy Thursday and Good Friday, the last supper and passion stories from John (chapters 11–19) are appropriate, and on Holy Saturday choose from *Genesis 5:32—8:22, Ezekiel 37: 1–14, Jonah 3:1–10, Daniel 3:1–24* and *Jeremiah 31:31–34.*

EASTER SEASON

During these 50 days, begin with the resurrection narratives in Matthew, chapter 28; Mark, chapter 16; Luke, chapter 24; and John, chapters 20–21. The Acts of the Apostles and Saint Peter's first letter will extend the story of the resurrection and its consequences. Also appropriate during the season is the entire gospel of John.

HYMNS FOR THE SEASONS

ABOUT THESE HYMNS

Brother Aelred-Seton Shanley, a lay Benedictine monk, composed these beautiful hymns for morning and evening prayer. Some are paraphrases of ancient texts or modern texts; others are original compositions. They are all long meter pieces (four-line stanzas, each line eight syllables) that may be recited as poetry or sung to the following familiar hymn tunes:

Old hundredth
> All people that on earth do dwell
> Praise God from whom all blessings flow

Erhalt uns herr
> Again we keep this solemn fast
> Lord, keep us steadfast in thy word

Puer nobis
> What star is this with beams so bright?

Emmanuel (without refrain)
> O come, O come, Emmanuel

Tallis canon
> All praise to thee, my God, this night

MORNINGS OF ADVENT

God's word which sounds throughout
   the world,
whose mercy wraps us round and round,
in John now finds an urgent voice:
"Repent! God's grace shall here abound!"

Relentless as the searing sun
yet gentle as the morning dew,
this voice cries in our wilderness:
"Receive the Gift; be born anew!"

The broken reed will Christ restore,
frail flames he'll fan to blazing fire;
with tenderness our wounds he'll bind,
the flock he shepherds, saved entire.

Anointed with the Spirit's pow'r,
he'll preach good news, make strong the weak,
demanding justice for the poor,
the basic rights that all would seek.

Our eyes, so blind, will see God's reign
revealed in those we once ignored;
our tongues that babble, gossip, rage
will speak out for the voiceless poor.

Lord Jesus, come: find us awake,
rehearsing now what is not yet.
This work of God, our works of God,
your glorious coming manifest! Amen.

EVENINGS OF ADVENT

O Myriam, prepare the day
when God takes shelter at your breast;
the Word, creation's source and end,
now with our features will take flesh.

The wedding chamber of your womb—
expectant, hallowed, fenced around—
grows full, so heavy now with child
whose name, "God heals," through earth
   will sound.

This Word, though birthless, comes to birth,
whose day the prophets strained to see.
Compassion, justice now embrace
and bare God's great fidelity.

You angel choirs, now mark the day:
prepare a new song for our earth.
God comes, self stripped of majesty
to die; but dying, gives us birth! Amen.

CHRISTMAS DAY TO EPIPHANY EVE MORNINGS

The root of Jesse now has flow'red
for Sarah's daughter bears a son!
Behold the Mother of our God
draws to her breast the Holy One.

The co-eternal Word of God
is cradled now in slumber deep:
he who holds planets to their course
now nestles in her arms, asleep.

The law which girds the universe,
God's Torah teaching Wisdom's ways,
in Mary, both have been enfleshed—
a source of scandal and God's praise.

This Jewish daughter's bold consent,
her wonderment, her "Let it be!"
has touched the very depths of God
and ever changed the way we see.

A contradiction to our time,
her single "Yes!" to what could be.
Have we such openness within
to bring the Word to birth as she? Amen.

CHRISTMAS EVE TO EPIPHANY EVE
EVENINGS

O Christ, in whom all is redeemed,
who shone before created light:
sprung from our Abba's boundless heart,
by God begotten God's delight!

Be mindful, Savior of our world,
you once were bound in swaddling bands,
and from a maiden's hallowed womb
you gave yourself into our hands.

The stars themselves shine bright as suns;
creation at its core is changed:
a wondrous new song fills the night,
the galaxies cannot contain!

With hearts made whole within your love,
we join this song of ransomed earth,
whose healing through your cross began
this hallowed night that saw your birth.

Most holy, moth'ring, fath'ring God,
be praised in Christ, your heart's delight:
come now in new nativity
and find your joy in us this night. Amen.

EPIPHANY TO BAPTISM OF THE LORD, MORNINGS AND EVENINGS

Famed though the world's great cities be,
yet none can Bethlehem excel,
for now there dawns God's deathless day
on Gentiles as on Israel.

More dazzling than the dawning sun,
this star that blazes at Christ's birth
proclaims to all the waiting world:
our God enfleshed upon this earth.

They who have listened to earth's ways,
who long have studied heaven's stars,
come seeking Wisdom's holy source—
their route a different one from ours.

Prostrate before the throne of grace,
they offer gifts both choice and rare:
gifts God first gave our mother earth,
her gold, her frankincense and myrrh.

Earth's sacred gifts speak mysteries:
incense God's holiness extolled,
God's sovereign realm the gold proclaimed,
but myrrh the cross and death foretold.

The magi, finding all they sought,
then traveled home a different way;
for nothing now remained the same
in light of what they found this day. Amen.

MORNINGS OF LENT

O sun of justice, thaw our hearts,
you draw the spring from earth's decay.
Then melt our safe complacency
which rests content with yesterday.

The "time acceptable" is now!
The dormant earth to growth gives way.
In prayer and fasting thaw our hearts;
let alms a world remade display.

You take us broken as we are,
and spread our dawning days with light;
may we rehearse your ways of love
till all we do gives you delight.

O everlasting Trinity,
we yearn to see that day of days
when all the earth, reborn again,
is vibrant with its Easter praise. Amen.

EVENINGS OF LENT

For forty days Christ fasted, fed
upon the Father's every word—
all for the joy that lay ahead;
such were his pleas, his prayer was heard.

Though one with God he plunged his heart
deep in the world's unfathomed pain;
he wrestled demons, hunger, thirst,
that we in him may do the same.

In Christ our journey is revealed:
his face set toward Jerusalem.
Where he, our head, goes, so must we:
the church, his body, one with him.

O Abba, food of those who fast,
O Christ in whom the least are known,
earth's rising sap, O Spirit-spring:
come raise to life what you have sown! Amen.

TRIDUUM
MORNINGS AND EVENINGS

Behold the cross, the tree of life,
where set the Sun whom we betrayed;
here he in flesh who fleshed our race,
our sentence bore, our ransom paid.

O barren wood, now bloodied, nailed,
you reek of human hate and scorn;
yet from you springs the shoot of life:
a new humanity is born.

O cross, the brand that sears our hearts,
our shame and strength, our ransom price!
This is God's Holy One you bear,
the Lamb, the paschal sacrifice.

O cross, traced deep upon your church,
embracing ev'ry sense and deed:
through you has Christ now harrowed hell
and from its clutches we are freed.

Immortal, holy, mighty God,
whose love for us the spear floods forth:
what love, self-emptied and outpoured,
is here consumed in holocaust.

O Trinity, you stoop to heal
the wounds of earth upon the cross:
all praise be yours as we proclaim
life's glorious rising and its source. Amen.

MORNINGS OF EASTER

Our justice, Christ, resplendent sun,
from prison tomb bursts forth in light;
within us joy and gladness dance
for Christ is risen in his might.

From death to life we have been raised,
from earth to heaven we are led:
for Christ our resurrection joy
is truly risen as he said.

Let all the heavens burst with joy,
let all the earth with song resound!
Let all creation join the dance
for Christ is risen, death is bound!

Come share the endless reign of Christ;
the hallowed chosen day has come!
Drink freely of the fresh new wine;
there's joy enough for everyone!

O Abba, Word and Spirit—spring
in whom we have been born anew,
our earth is filled with paschal praise;
ours is the joy in hymning you. Amen.

EVENINGS OF EASTER

Come one and all, white-robed and washed,
the banquet of the Lamb is spread!
Our exodus is at an end:
proclaim Christ risen from the dead!

For death our blood-stained doors did pass
that night we fled our slavery;
of our oppressors, none survived,
while we passed dry-shod through the sea.

Our Moses, Christ! Our guide, our pasch
whose blood has sanctified us all:
our paschal bread, sincere and true,
whose fragrance fills the wedding hall.

O Word of God, for us enfleshed,
whom we betrayed, for silver sold:
you suffered death, yet loved us still
to give us life a hundredfold.

Hell is no more; its sov'reign head,
deceiving death, is dragged in tow.
You raise us to our Abba's throne,
with all the dead whose names you know.

With boundless love the feast is laid,
yet never did you count the cost!
Our savior, priest and sacrifice—
our shepherd shoulders now the lost! Amen.

MORNING OF PENTECOST

Christ's friends with Mary gather now,
united, one in heart and home;
in prayer they wait the promised gift,
receptive now to God's unknown.

The primal cosmic breath and fire
envelops them with searing pow'r:
creation's birth and Sinai's blaze
both consummated in this hour.

Each one God's holy temple now,
they speak of all they saw and heard;
with new-found tongues they now proclaim
what to the world will seem absurd.

Intoxicated by new wine,
still sober even as they reel,
their former sadness is displaced
by God's own joy, the Spirit's seal!

She forms new hearts and law within,
a new creation fashioning:
have we new eyes, new ways to see
her holiness in everything? Amen.

EVENING OF PENTECOST

Come now, creating Spirit, come!
Create new worlds and make our hearts
as boundless and as infinite
as is the life your breath imparts!

O gift transcending all we have!
O wondrous, deep, consummate love!
Wellspring of life and searing flame,
our christ'ning into Christ above!

Yours is the open hand of God
whence come new gifts as each has need,
our Abba's promised advocate
when words cannot contain our plea.

Transfuse our every sense with light,
well up in love both bold and pure;
forge us in solidarity
with what the world holds weak and poor.

Through you we know our Abba-God,
through you we know the risen One.
You are their loving, lovely love
at play before all was begun! Amen.

BASIC PRAYERS

ABOUT PRAYER

For Christians, prayer is partly learned and partly received as a gift from God. We learn to pray by using normal human efforts to repeat the consecrated texts of our tradition. With persistent use, these verbal forms of prayer support and enrich our personal ways of speaking to God from our hearts.

But prayer is also a gift. In the sacraments of Christian initiation the Holy Spirit is poured out in our hearts and there cries to God continuously, "Abba, dear Father" (Galatians 4:6). The Spirit praying within us is an irresistible impulse toward God, although we can become dull to its promptings.

We have the very breath of God pulsating in us, urging us toward the invisible Presence. We have also received a set of basic prayers to memorize and use every day as channels for the Spirit's power: the Sign of the Cross, the Apostles' Creed, the Lord's Prayer, the Hail Mary, the doxologies and others. Along with the psalms and canticles of the Bible, these are gifts of the Spirit coming to us through our church's tradition. By way of parents, catechists and friends, our faith community hands over these prayers to us, sometimes orally, sometimes through books.

THE SIGN OF THE CROSS

The church imposes on us this essential sign in baptism and confirmation and we use it in many ways: to sign our lips to open them in praise; to sign our forehead, lips and heart at the reading of the gospel; to sign our children on their foreheads at bedtime. We sign our whole body, from head to heart and from left to right shoulder, as a shield of faith and an act of commitment and rededication to Christ. As we begin morning and evening prayer, we make the sign of the cross on our lips, often with the words, "O Lord, open my lips . . ." We use the full sign of the cross at the end of these hours and also when beginning the gospel canticles of Zachary (at morning prayer), Mary (at evening prayer) and Simeon (at night prayer). When the sign of the cross is used on other occasions, the words are always these:

In the name + of the Father,
and of the Son,
and of the Holy Spirit. Amen.

THE APOSTLES' CREED

This basic profession of the Christian faith is given to us in baptism. It originated in the profession of faith that was made at Rome as new Christians were immersed three times in the baptismal pool in the name of the three persons of the Trinity. Through the Creed, we renew our baptismal vows committing us to Christ and his gospel.

I believe in God, the Father almighty,
   creator of heaven and earth.

I believe in Jesus Christ, God's only Son, our Lord,
   who was conceived by the Holy Spirit,
   born of the Virgin Mary,
   suffered under Pontius Pilate,
   was crucified, died, and was buried;
   he descended to the dead.
   On the third day he rose again;
   he ascended into heaven,
   he is seated at the right hand of the Father,
   and he will come to judge the living and the dead.

I believe in the Holy Spirit,
   the holy catholic church,
   the communion of saints,
   the forgiveness of sins,
   the resurrection of the body,
   and the life everlasting. Amen.

THE LORD'S PRAYER

Often called simply the "Our Father," this prayer, too, is a gift of the Holy Spirit praying in us. The Lord Jesus himself taught it to his first disciples (Matthew 6:9–13, Luke 11:1–4) and the church put it on our lips in baptism and authorized and empowered us to say it as children of God. The earliest recorded instance of its use is in the Didache, *a late-first-century document that tells us to say the Lord's Prayer three times a day.*

This beautiful prayer gives us words to pray and also a model for all of our prayers. It shows us how to pray and what to pray for.

OLDER VERSION

Our Father, who art in heaven,
   hallowed be thy name;
   thy kingdom come;
   thy will be done on earth as it is in heaven.
Give us this day our daily bread;
   and forgive us our trespasses
   as we forgive those who trespass against us;
   and lead us not into temptation,
   but deliver us from evil.

For the kingdom, the power, and the glory are yours,
   now and for ever. Amen.

MODERN VERSION

Our Father in heaven,
   hallowed be your name,
   your kingdom come,
   your will be done, on earth as in heaven.
Give us today our daily bread.
Forgive us our sins
   as we forgive those who sin against us.
Save us from the time of trial
   and deliver us from evil.

For the kingdom, the power, and the glory are yours,
now and for ever. Amen.

HAIL MARY

*The Hail Mary is a combination of two texts in the
gospel of Luke (1:26–45). In the first part the Archangel
Gabriel salutes the Virgin Mary (verse 28) and in the
second part her cousin Elizabeth, the mother of John
the Baptist, moved by the Holy Spirit, hails her as
doubly blessed (verse 42). The third part of the Hail
Mary was developed in the late Middle Ages.*

Hail, Mary, full of grace, the Lord is with you.
Blessed are you among women,
and blessed is the fruit of your womb, Jesus.
Holy Mary, Mother of God, pray for us sinners,
now and at the hour of our death. Amen.

THE *ANGELUS*

*In the thirteenth century, the brothers of Saint Francis
of Assisi (1181–1226) began to recite a daily set of
prayers in honor of the Word-made-Flesh and of
Mary's free consent to God's loving initiative. This
custom spread to the whole Latin church and is sig-
naled by a peal of bells at 6 AM, 12 noon and 6 PM.
This devotion is especially suitable to the noon hour
each day.*

The angel of the Lord brought the good news
   to Mary.
~*And she conceived by the Holy Spirit.*

Hail, Mary, full of grace, the Lord is with you.
Blessed are you among women
and blessed is the fruit of your womb, Jesus.
~*Holy Mary, Mother of God, pray for us sinners,*
now and at the hour of our death. Amen.

"I am the Lord's servant.
~*May it happen to me as you have said."*
Hail, Mary . . .

And the Word was made flesh.
~*And dwelt among us.*
Hail Mary . . .

Pray for us, O holy Mother of God.
~*That we may become worthy of the promises*
of Christ.

Let us pray:
Pour forth, O Lord,
your grace into our hearts
that we to whom the incarnation of Christ
   your Son
was made known by the message of an angel,
may by his passion and cross be brought
to the glory of his resurrection.
Through the same Christ our Lord.
~*Amen.*

THE *REGINA CAELI*

During the Fifty Days of Easter, this twelfth-century Marian anthem replaces the Angelus each day.

Rejoice, O Queen of heaven, alleluia!
for the Son you bore, alleluia!
has arisen as he promised, alleluia!
Pray for us to God the Father, alleluia!

Rejoice and be glad, O Virgin, Mary, alleluia!
~For the Lord has truly risen, alleluia!

Let us pray:
Holy and deathless God,
you have given joy to the world
by the resurrection of your Son,
    our Lord Jesus Christ.
Through the prayers of his mother,
   the Virgin Mary,
bring us to the happiness of eternal life.
We ask this through Christ our Lord.
~Amen.

THE JESUS PRAYER

One of the oldest, simplest and best of prayers is a calling in faith upon the Holy Name of Jesus. By repeatedly invoking the name of our Savior, we penetrate more deeply and surely into a growing awareness of the presence of God who saves and sanctifies us from within.

The Holy Name is sometimes repeated by itself and sometimes in a phrase. The most common form of the fuller invocation is:

Lord Jesus Christ, Son of the living God,
have mercy on me, a sinner.

The best way to say the Jesus Prayer is to sit in as much physical and inner stillness as one can manage and then repeat the invocation over and over, slowly and steadily, fixing the mind directly and intensely on the words of the prayer itself, without trying to conjure up any mental pictures or intellectual concepts.

Persistent, frequent attempts to pray in this way will gradually habituate the soul to more effortless and continuous use of the Holy Name until it becomes the very substance of one's life of prayer. It is well to use the Jesus Prayer before and after other forms of prayer, such as the forms of morning and evening prayer contained in this prayer book. It can also be used during normal intervals in the day's work, when walking from place to place, for example, even when conditions are not ideal for recollected kinds of prayer.

The Jesus Prayer is an act of faith and self-surrender to the indwelling Spirit who longs to teach us to pray without ceasing. It is a path to contemplative prayer and to "the peace that passes all understanding" (Philippians 4:7).

Acknowledgments continued from page iv

Psalms passages from *The Psalms: Grail Translation from the Hebrew* © 1993 by Ladies of the Grail (England). Used by permission of GIA Publications, Inc., exclusive agent. All rights reserved.

Scripture reading, p. 115, from The Revised Common Lectionary in *Readings for the Assembly,* New Revised Standard Version, Emended. Minneapolis: Augsburg Fortress, ©1997.

English translations of the following items prepared by the English Language Liturgical Consultation (ELLC) found in *Praying Together,* Abingdon Press: 1988: The Canticle of Zachary, pp. 12–13, 41–42, 116–17, 143–44, 233–34, The Canticle of Mary, pp. 6, 17–18, 27–28, 45–46, 64, 87–88, 98–99, 110–11, 132–33, 138, 148–49, 212, 237–38, 295–96, The Canticle of Simeon, pp. 36, 77, 121 and The Canticle of the Church, pp. 88–89 (used for Intercessions), 221–22, 252–53, The Canticle of the Heavenly Host, pp. 83–84, the Apostles' Creed, p. 324 and the modern version of the Lord's Prayer, pp. 325–26.

Scripture passages, pp. 179, 270–71, 281–82, from the *Good News Translation,* 2nd edition; Today's English Version © 1992. American Bible Society. Used by permission.

All other scripture excerpts are from the *New Revised Standard Version Bible* ©1989 Division of Christian Education of the National Council for the Churches of Christ in the United States of America. Used by permission. All rights reserved.

Father, source of light, p. 96: from the *Roman Missal* © 1973, International Committee on English in the Liturgy, Inc. All rights reserved.

Canticles, pp. 128–29, 152–53, 157, 206–7, 262, from *A New Zealand Prayer Book* He Karakia Mihinare o Aotearoa. Aukland: Collins, 1989. Copyright material taken from this book is used with permission.

Prayer, pp. 134–35, from *The Stanbrook Abbey Hymnal,* © Stanbrook Abbey, 1974.

It was John's mission, p. xx, *The Lord* by Romano Guardini. Chicago: Henry Regnery, © 1954, p. 24.

The church repeats, p. 123, in *Seasons of Grace* by Pius Parsch trans. by H. E. Winstone. New York: Herder and Herder © 1963, pp. 141, 144.

What a strange, p. 214, in *The Awe-Inspiring Rites of Initiation* by Edward Yarnold, 2d. ed. Collegeville, MN: The Liturgical Press, 1994, pp. 78, 80.

Our Lord Jesus Christ, p. 199, in *Selected Easter Sermons of Saint Augustine,* trans. and commentary by Philip T. Weller. St. Louis: B. Herder Book Co., p. 82.